HOW YOU CAN TURN YOUR TALENTS AND POTENTIAL INTO LASTING SUCCESS

BOOST

CHRIS WISDOM

RETHINK PRESS

Published in Great Britain 2013
by Rethink Press (www.rethinkpress.com)

© Copyright Chris Wisdom

All rights reserved. No part of this publication may be reproduced, stored in or introduced into a retrieval system, or transmitted, in any form, or by any means (electronic, mechanical, photocopying, recording or otherwise) without the prior written permission of the publisher.

This book is sold subject to the condition that it shall not, by way of trade or otherwise, be lent, resold, hired out, or otherwise circulated without the publisher's prior consent in any form of binding or cover other than that in which it is published and without a similar condition including this condition being imposed on the subsequent purchaser.

PRAISE FOR BOOST!

'Guaranteed to give you that needed Boost! for lasting success, Chris Wisdom's insights will motivate you to take action today!'

Marshall Goldsmith
The Thinkers50 Award Winner (by Harvard Business Review)
for Most-Influential Leadership Thinker in the World

'It mustn't be easy being born with "Wisdom" as your last name; clearly it creates expectations. This book lives up to those expectations because it is a powerhouse of tips, tactics and approaches that simply work. Powerful, practical and solid advice for success. A fantastic book.'

Daniel Priestley
Entrepreneur and Best-selling author of
Key Person of Influence and *Entrepreneur Revolution*

'This book redefines practically what a successful career should look like in today's business world. Reading the book gives you a thinking framework for putting things in perspective that is both therapeutic and energetic.'

Jo Benoit
General Manager France, Benelux at Baxter Healthcare

'*Boost!* brings together those key fundamentals that will enable you to use your talents to their fullest. Chris gives you a complete picture of success. It's about you, your relationships and actions that make it happen.'

Mark Fritz
International Speaker, Visiting Professor, Author & Mentor:
Get More Ownership from your Teams around the World

'Success is not just for the lucky or privileged few. It *can* be learned by anyone and this book will show you how.'

Paul Newton
Chief Legal Officer, BUPA

'A simple, practical, life-giving handbook acting as your personal coach for life: here are the basics for living and working well. From the wise arts of communication to managing yourself, Chris Wisdom's easy-read and supportive style will ask you questions and *Boost!* you with solutions and tactics to strengthen your mindset and creativity for life and work.'

Mike Thompson
Professor of Management Practice,
China Europe International Business School, Shanghai

'Comprehensive advice, support and challenge from an exceptional executive coach. Chris has distilled his professional and personal experience into a really useful book.'

Craig Scott
Managing Director, Tata Steel Projects

FOREWORD

Most of us want to be better. For some it's about changing aspects of our lives that frustrate and dissatisfy us. For some it's about reaching out for something more. But not everyone does something about it. The very fact that you have picked this book up and got this far indicates you want a boost.

Well, you'll get a boost when you read this book because Chris Wisdom is someone who has worked these ideas out in his own life and communicates them well to others. I can say this because I have seen the working out and the working through over many years in the way Chris lives and I have benefitted personally and professionally by what he communicates and the way he communicates it.

The personal benefit? At a pivotal moment in my life I benefitted from Chris's wisdom. I had experienced heady success and then dramatic failure in my business life and I badly needed to find a way forward. Chris listened as I talked and was remarkably patient and compassionate. But he also challenged me to change my thinking in the way I saw myself and then (very practically) to stick with a course of action that was very tough at the time, but which has produced good and long-lasting fruit in my life.

The professional benefit? I spend a good deal of my time working with people who need to lead high-value relationships on behalf of major financial institutions and professional service firms. On almost every occasion I speak I use Chris as an example in one of two areas. First I talk about the need to listen. I ask people to think of someone to whom they are willing to open up, whom they really trust. Then I ask them to reflect on the characteristics of that person. 'What is about them that makes you willing to be open and not to play a game, pretending to be open but in fact holding back?' I then describe some of Chris' characteristics as a listener and a coach and we conclude that if we could exhibit some of these characteristics our business relationships would be more open and more productive. I've seen the impact of Chris' approach on these professionals and you'll read about them in this book.

The second place I see the impact of Chris' input is when I talk about effective teams. I describe a team that Chris led and I was part of. We were a diverse group of strong characters. We had a clear purpose but faced real challenges. I describe the characteristics of the team and the way Chris led us. It was the best team I have been involved in. Again, you'll read about effective ways of working on yourself and engaging with others.

So, having benefitted from Chris' approach both personally and professionally I was delighted to hear he had written *Boost!* and asked if I could write a recommendation. I am honoured that Chris has asked me to write this foreword. As I read the book, Chris revealed new things to me – things I simply hadn't thought of. He has reminded me of things I know in theory but don't always put into practice, and he reassured me that change is possible and lies in my hands.

I enjoyed this book. It has made a difference to me and I have great pleasure in recommending it to you! It's a practical book and I urge you to take Chris' practical ideas and use the tools he provides to give yourself a real boost!

Richard Higham MA FRSA
Global Practice Leader Financial & Professional Services
Mercuri International

CONTENTS

INTRODUCTION   1

Part 1 ZIP: BOOST! Yourself

1   Pause – Turn your talents into lasting success   9

2   Choose – Get everything you want   17

3   Dream – Unlock the might of your imagination   26

4   Shine – Enjoy your journey and avoid the pitfalls   34

5   Focus – Make action plans not wish lists   42

6   ZIP – Get mountains of motivation   50

STOP – GROW – FLOW Chart (1)   57

Part 2 PEP: BOOST! Your Relationships

7   Adapt – Why listening makes life easy   61

8   Attract – Profit from the art of persuasion   70

9   Give – Give and you'll succeed   78

10   Push – Stand up for yourself   86

11   Swerve – Stop working the hard way   93

12   Sparkle – Do it with style   101

13   PEP – Why it pays to make others look good   111

STOP – GROW – FLOW Chart (2)   119

Part 3 ZOOM: BOOST! Your Skills

14   Start – The secrets of sustaining your performance   123

15   Stop – Become time rich   132

16   Plan – Create a course for certain super-productivity   140

17 Achieve – Make an unforgettable positive impact   148

18 Play – Renew your joy and become one of the great explorers   155

19 Think – Stretch your mind and make your brain big   165

20 Speak – Master the power of presenting   173

21 ZOOM – Why stay on the launchpad when you could be in orbit?   180

STOP – GROW – FLOW Chart (3)   186

THE AUTHOR   **188**

DEDICATION

This book is dedicated to my incomparable wife, Rose. Without her invaluable, never ending encouragement and support it simply wouldn't have happened.

It's also for my wonderful children, Sophie, Emmy and Jake, because it is the book I wanted to write for them as they look forward to an exciting and successful future.

Everyday I appreciate my mum, still going strong, and Dad (who died too young) because they instilled in me a genuine desire to encourage other people. Their example of helping others is one of the main reasons I do what I do.

And it's for my brother Andrew who personifies many of the principles here in his own business and service in his community.

Success comes in many forms and your idea of it is the most important for you.

INTRODUCTION

The person who really wants to do something finds a way; others find an excuse.

E.C. MCKENZIE

Fit for your future

When I decided it was time to get fitter I bought a mountain bike. Smart move. Well, not so much. I was a bit overweight. I didn't have a great diet and hadn't exercised strenuously for quite a while. I quickly discovered, after some uncomfortable encounters with hills (you couldn't call them mountains) resulting in very sore muscles where I didn't know I had muscles, that I needed to get fit to go mountain biking rather than go mountain biking to get fit!

To enjoy the sport and reach my potential I was going to have to stop my bad eating habits, take seriously losing weight and improve my fitness overall. In short, there were things I would have to *stop* and *change* before I could *reach* new levels of fitness and achieve goals I would not have thought possible when I started. I began to work with a personal trainer and it became clear that I needed to work on three things at the same time – *nutrition, exercise* and *rest*.

Putting these ideas together, I would have to *stop, change* and *reach new levels* for each of these three areas. I remember the process as simply, Stop – Grow – Flow. For example, as far as nutrition was concerned I needed to:

- Stop – Eating and drinking so much of the wrong foods
- Grow – Begin to learn what healthy and energy giving foods to eat
- Flow* – Make this new way of eating a lifestyle not a short-term fix

This is important because if you don't use a process and make a long-term commitment, it is so easy to go backwards and lose the benefits of all the hard work you've put in. You see this most commonly when people try the latest fad diet, but it also happens with personal and professional development. The people who stop the bad habits, make the changes and make them stick are the ones who progress and really achieve their ambitions.

(* Mihaly Csikszentmihalyi wrote a book called *Flow*. He described 'flow' as a state when you are fully immersed in something, energised and positive. It occurs when you are consistently challenging your skills to a high level.)

Achieve lasting success

In my career I have coached, trained and educated hundreds of people for thousands of hours on the theme of what it takes to turn their talents and potential into lasting success – people from many different types of organisation: very big businesses, medium sized companies and small firms, public sector and one-person enterprises. Many of them are very senior and others are full of potential and aspiring to advance in their businesses and careers. People like you.

I have observed those who go from strength to strength and also those who plateau or, worse, derail and never fulfil their potential or get the rewards they could have.

→ Lasting success

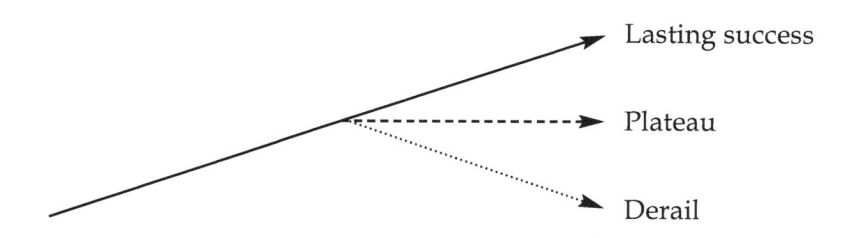

------→ Plateau

↘ Derail

Those who achieve growing and lasting success are those who pay the greatest attention to becoming excellent. It's not an accident. They are eager to learn how they can improve, are enthusiastic for feedback and dedicated to personal learning and professional growth. What I have observed is that they work on three areas at the same time, whatever stage they have reached. They work on themselves, their relationships and their skills. What's important is different at different stages, but the principle remains true.

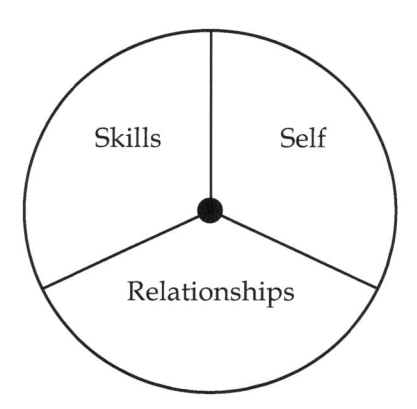

Skills | Self | Relationships

I've also observed what happens when it doesn't go well – the people who plateau or derail. I see the thinking and attitudes, unconscious habits, unintentional mistakes and challenges that result in stress, lack of fulfilment and disappointment. This isn't because of a lack of talent, potential or intelligence; often it is just because people don't know what or how to make the changes that will result in the achievements and success they want and deserve.

INTRODUCTION | 3

This book combines the practical knowledge, tools and systems I have built through my work, the experiences of others and my own extensive reading over more than 20 years. It contains the keys to how you can achieve growing and lasting success and pitfalls you can avoid. This book gives you the inspiration, stimulation, ideas and answers to help you excel. There are lots of quick wins giving you results now, but you'll also be able to use them for the rest of your life. It is written in three parts with short chapters. At the end of each chapter you'll find a *Big Mental Note* to remind you of a key thought; and *One Small Step* to encourage you to choose one action to get you started. These are suggestions and you might choose something else. At the end of each part is a page for you to collate your ideas for how you will apply *Stop, Grow, Flow* for that part of the book.

In Part One, each chapter builds on the last, so it is a good idea to read these consecutively. In Parts Two and Three, the chapters stand alone more, so you can pick and choose what seems most relevant to you, but remember there may be hidden gems in unexpected places.

Part One helps you develop your personal vision, momentum and focus. Many things will come along to divert you and block your path both from inside you and outside, but when you grasp and apply these principles you'll keep powering forward.

Part Two elevates you to the level of expert in working with others. You'll know how to influence and collaborate with others so that you can bring the best out of them and win them over. You'll also know how to handle others' behaviour when it could knock you off course.

Part Three gives you a carefully selected set of skills that you need to excel in if you are going to be outstanding and stay ahead of the game in a local-global market. The tools are quick and easy to apply and can reward your effort immediately, repeatedly and throughout your life.

3 x 3 = Growing and Lasting Success

All you need to keep in mind as you read each chapter is this simple 3 x 3 model.

Self + Relationships + Skills x Stop + Grow + Flow

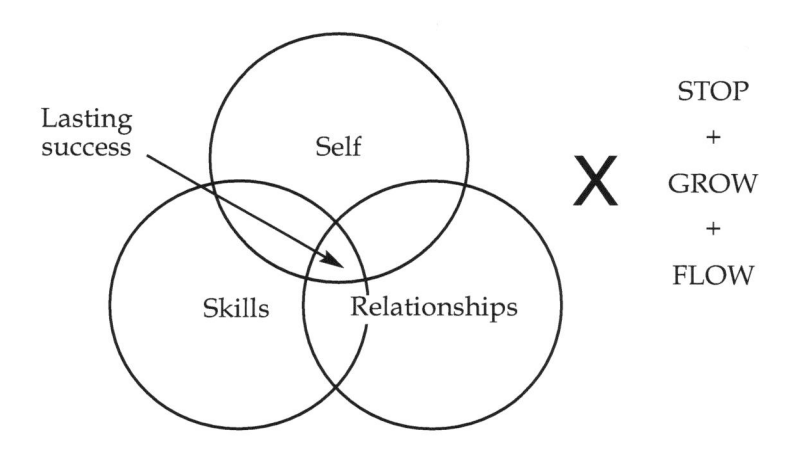

```
          Self
Lasting
success ──► 
    Skills  Relationships
```

X

STOP
+
GROW
+
FLOW

Why *BOOST!* ?

This is my passion. This book is intended to be challenging and practical, but most of all encouraging. I hope this book BOOSTS! you, your career, your fulfilment, your success and your bank balance.

INTRODUCTION | 5

PART 1
ZIP
BOOST! Yourself

1 | PAUSE

Turn your talent into lasting success

In the end it is important to remember that we cannot become what we need to be by remaining what we are.

MAX DE PREE

What's holding you back?

This morning at the gym, when I was using some weights, a trainer came to help me. I know this is hard to believe – usually they just strut around looking gorgeous and making the rest of us feel inadequate. But today was different.

He asked if I would mind if he worked with me on my technique. He demonstrated how the way I was performing an exercise was not going to give me the results I wanted and there was the risk of injury. I'd formed some bad habits.

He said, 'The problem with us guys is we get all macho and want to do heavier and heavier weights!'

'Moi?' I said.

He told me to stop loading on so many weights and do the exercise using a better technique. All I needed was an adjustment to what I was already doing to improve the results massively.

You can be educated, talented and smart, but it doesn't guarantee lasting success. You can fulfil your potential by choosing to do the right things or you can assume you are good enough and fall short. Remaining as you are is not an option because people with as much or less talent, but greater awareness, passion and commitment, will pass you by. You'll miss out. You can read this as a huge book of personal feedback, which will help you to get more success, more easily and enjoy it more all at the same time. The only thing that can ultimately hold you back is you. Now is the time to decide to commit to keep growing and developing every day. Then your talents will truly shine and keep shining.

Lack of success is just a bad habit

The way to get more of the success you want more easily is not a great mystery. You don't need to understand your star chart, delve into the depths of your psyche or have better luck. The secret to getting more of the success you want is to do more consistently those things which will bring you that success. That's what this book is about. Using the process I describe will make this much easier for you.

In a speech first delivered to life insurance professionals in 1940, Albert Gray said, 'If you do not deliberately form good habits then *unconsciously* you will form bad ones.' He observed life insurance sales people who were failures and those who were successes and he saw the forming of good habits as absolutely key to success. It wasn't their height, sparkling smile or even their intelligence. It was the way that they went about their work that guaranteed their success.

You've probably formed many good habits, but there is a good chance that you will have unconsciously formed bad ones as well and they could be holding you back. The trick is to notice what is working for you, and do it even better and more consistently, but also to become aware of, and acknowledge, what's holding you back. The great news is that habits can be changed.

Good habits can be made even more powerful, new ones can be learned and poor habits can be eliminated. Whether it is about the way you think, how you interact with others or your everyday skills and capabilities, you can stop doing the things that are holding you back and do more of those things that will bring you the rewards and achievements you desire.

Don't blame me I'm unconscious

This simple diagram gives you a picture of how you learn, but it also shows how you develop good habits as well as some bad ones. If you think you know how to interpret it – think again, because the usual understanding could mislead you. If you consider learning to drive a car, using some new software, or anything else that involves a bit of effort to get the hang of, the idea is that you move from Box 1 through 2 and 3 to Box 4. By the time you reach Box 4 you've really mastered the skill.

1. Unconscious Incompetence	2. Conscious Incompetence
3. Conscious Competence	4. Unconscious Competence

Think about the example of learning to drive. Box 1 indicates your fist attempts when you are a complete beginner. Warnings should be sent out to all other road users that you are out there. You know so little that you don't even know what you don't know and you can't even do that right!

Box 2 shows that you are making some progress. You have learned enough to know what you are doing wrong. Your skill level hasn't yet caught up. You know what you are doing wrong at least some of the time, but the chances you'll create mayhem are still pretty high.

Box 3 is the state of hyper-concentration you are in when you take your practical test. You are thinking about everything you know, everything you've practised and everything you've been told, and are desperately trying to demonstrate it perfectly for the examiner whilst remaining calm, controlled and not too sweaty.

Box 4 represents the level of performance where you drive competently without having to think about it.

But that word 'unconscious' has always worried me, especially when it is applied to driving! If there is any time you don't want to be unconscious it's when you are at the wheel. It is generally regarded as one of those things people get touchy about. You are competent in so far as you can operate the car, but if you stop thinking about how you are operating the car you are headed for big trouble.

The problem with Unconscious Competence is it can so easily become Unconscious Incompetence. Many so-called experienced drivers would struggle to pass their test again because they have developed so many bad habits of which they may or may not be aware. Good drivers concentrate pretty hard on driving well. Successful people concentrate hard on doing the important things right, every day and every time. That's called Conscious Competence.

Successful people pay a lot of attention to their own development. Sometimes the idea of being coached or trained as a business person can be seen as an admission of failure, but the most successful sports people and those who are aspiring to be successful in all walks of life often have several people coaching them in different aspects of their profession. They don't settle because they know that as soon as they do they'll lose their touch and become vulnerable to the competition.

Break out of your comfort zone

I assume you have many strengths. I know you do. You are an amazing human being. You also have enormous potential and room to grow. One of the things that can hold you back is your attachment to your bad practices. As crazy as it seems, you get attached to your bad habits. Even when they are not doing you any good, you often prefer to stay the way you are rather than change. It's called homeostasis, which means a state of equilibrium. Yes! Even when it's not working for you it's often easier to just stay the way you are. Just look around and you'll see the results of this in others who have habits they want to change, but never do.

Why are you like this? Because it is comfortable. That's why you know the phrase 'comfort zone'. It is the zone that requires the least effort, disruption and change. This is why some people don't really change anything for years until an event outside their control forces them to. People are made redundant or have an accident or life-threatening experience, and then they make a real change. Why does this happen? It's all because of your comfort zone. You are more comfortable being the way you are and doing things the way you are doing them. It is, of course, easier not to challenge yourself. It is easier to stay settled.

But why wait for near death experiences or financial worries before you do something? Why settle for less than you could have? This is a manifesto to challenge yourself to get the best out of yourself and your job. To do work in a way that is enjoyable, fulfilling and a lot more rewarding. What does this mean for you if you want to grow and develop and be even more successful and fulfilled? Simply this – you've got to really, really want to! You'll read more about this in Chapter 5, but for now just think about this question: 'Do I really, really want to fulfil my potential, whatever it takes?'

You don't need to feel pressure to fix everything all in one go. It is usually counter-productive anyway. It is best to focus on one thing or a few things. Start thinking about those things that could be holding you back from achieving the success and happiness you want and deserve. Some of these habits can be hard to break and you might decide to find a coach or mentor who can help you through the barriers and challenges, but there's plenty here to get you going in the right direction.

If you are feeling uncertain of the next steps; if you are wondering how to progress to the next stage, that's okay. Those feelings of dissatisfaction are the beginning of growth and breakthrough. Don't ignore them. Accept the discomfort and use it to energise yourself to move on.

Pause for thought

If you want more success and fulfilment, go through this process first. Pause for thought. More and more is being asked of fewer people with the expectation of even greater performance. Even if the pressure isn't coming from your boss, customers or others, you can feel inwardly pressured to achieve and demand more and more of yourself.

Keeping your business moving forward, whether you are running your own or as part of a greater enterprise, requires more knowledge, more time and more expertise than ever. There will always be a good reason not to stop.

Time out!

Whatever you do, don't just carry on thoughtlessly. You might think, 'I don't have the time to think about this', but that's how you risk wasting your time, your talent and your potential. I know someone who is in a senior position in his company, but hates his job. He has hated it for years and can't wait to leave. That's how work becomes monotonous, too stressful and can suck the life out of you instead of being the mixture of learning, enjoyment, reward and performance that it can be. That's when you just start living for the weekend. Instead of living the breadth of your life you are just living the length of it.

Apply the brakes

Did you ever have that experience as a child when you were on a bicycle, peddling harder and faster going downhill, the wobbling started and you lost your balance? I once managed to cycle straight into a wall using that highly suspect technique. I had failed to master steering and using the brakes.

That's what can happen when you get so absorbed. You can lose direction, momentum and equilibrium.

You may have fallen into the trap of thinking that if you work harder and harder and fulfil all the demands, things are bound to improve. Working harder, faster and longer doesn't necessarily make you more productive or wise. Clearly, hard work is a big part of success, but only if you are working hard on the right things in the right way; only if it's making you more effective and productive; and only if it is propelling you quickly toward your goals and the kind of work you love doing.

Lots of noise, little progress?

On a recent holiday, I hired a car with a fundamental problem. When I pressed my foot on the accelerator there was a lot of noise, the rev counter shot up, but the speed increased negligibly. Eventually there was a sudden surge of power (surge may be overstating it), which rapidly diminished, then the car settled into a speed marginally greater than before the sequence started only to lose that speed rapidly. This was supposed to be an economy vehicle, but so much energy was expended because of the inefficiency it kept running out of fuel. Sound familiar? No not your car – you. It's an analogy!

Then (back to cars) there are those glorious models that just sweep down the highway. Some people seem to be able to do things differently. They have purpose, poise and energy and still deliver. They achieve their goals, deliver on time, delight their customers, keep fit and have a fulfilling personal life as well. They volunteer for charities, climb mountains and save children from burning buildings all without breaking into a sweat.

Don't mistake activity and busyness for progress and meaningful work. Lots of noise doesn't necessarily mean you are going anywhere fast. Being busy, stressed and tired out doesn't mean it is worth it. I clearly remember the day when I realised I felt overworked and frantic without being stretched. I knew I wasn't learning or growing; I knew I wasn't getting the pleasure, rewards and experiences I longed for and it was up to me to do something about it.

Look in the mirror

Decide today that you are going to do what it takes. Stop doing those things that aren't working for you, break out of your comfort zone and learn the new things that will enable you to grow and get to the next level and beyond. When you take a step back from the constant on-the-go-ness to evaluate the way you are doing what you are doing, you have taken a huge positive step forward. The rest of this book is going to highlight the vital thinking, attitudes, skills and capabilities that will enable you to take a step up, fulfil much more of your potential and leave the competition standing. It will give you the tools and models which, when you use them consciously, consistently and well, will give you more of the success you want.

If you haven't realised already, I'm not encouraging you to look around at your circumstances, your past or other people to discover what's holding you back from getting to the next level. The first place to look is yourself. You are a gifted and unique person and your success lies in using your talents, knowledge, experience and skills to the fullest. The best way to do that is to take personal and full responsibility for your own progress right now.

> **BIG MENTAL NOTE**
>
> *Remaining as you are is not an option because people with less talent,* but *greater awareness, passion and commitment will pass you by.*
>
> | ONE SMALL STEP |
>
> *Think about one thing you already do well and what holds you back from being outstanding.*

2 | CHOOSE

Get everything you want

The best way to predict your future is to create it.
PETER F. DRUCKER

Invest in yourself

Drivers select the destination, choose the route, decide on the speed, have the skills to get there and know what to do if there is a problem. They can take action and even make choices for other people. Drivers are active. Passengers are passive. They are dependent on drivers to get them where they want to go. Passengers need drivers, but drivers rarely need passengers. Which one are you?

A friend once challenged me that if you don't have your own plan you are part of someone else's plan. If you don't have your own jigsaw you are just a piece in someone else's jigsaw. You get the idea. It's a little bit like the game in the park when someone gets upset and decides to take their ball home. No ball, no game – if you don't have your own ball.

The business writer Charles Handy shares a story of when he was waiting outside the door of 'Personnel' in the company where he worked. An older Scottish colleague walked by and asked what he was waiting for. When he replied, 'I am waiting to see what they have planned for me', the Scot said, 'Invest in yourself, my boy, don't wait for them. Invest in yourself; if you don't, why should they?' If you are employed by a large organisation or even if you are part of a smaller enterprise or your own boss, this attitude is fundamental to your progress and fulfilment.

The way the large organisation looks after you can seem reassuring and affirming, but what happens when they make choices that aren't what you'd have chosen for yourself? In smaller organisations it can be even easier to end up doing the wrong thing because there's usually less choice. Perhaps surprisingly, even when you are self-employed lack of clarity about what sort of work you want to do and what type of clients you want to work with can mean that you find yourself working in a way that is more stressful and less fulfilling than the job you left.

If you don't design your life, someone else will do it for you and you may not like the choices they make. Have you got your own ball? Time to get your own ball again, or for the very first time.

Keep your eye on the ball

Many careers, businesses and other enterprises start with huge amounts of optimism. Initially you may just be glad to get a job or pleased to have made those first steps in working on our own thing, but if you aren't crystal clear about what you want then bad things can begin to happen.

You begin to give away your personal power and at that point, you begin to become dependent on your employer, your boss, your customers or your circumstances for the path you can take or the options you have. Who is narrowing your options for you? Who is making your choices?

When you start out, nobody warns you about this.

Work and careers are considered a means to an end. If you can get a good job and preferably a career, you will be able to earn a good income and get and do all the things you want outside work. Nobody told you that what you do, the way you do it and who you do it with are critical to your happiness and fulfilment and therefore your quality of life. They don't tell you that having a lovely home, impressive car and gadgets will not be enough to enable you to really enjoy your life and work if your work is not itself enriching, challenging and rewarding in your eyes.

For a while, the sacrifice you are making seems to be justified, but it doesn't last. Have you noticed how easily this turns into blame or inertia? Inwardly you begin blaming others for your lack of opportunity or the type of work you are doing. Inertia sets in because you can't see a way out or you feel you've run out of options. Who or what are you blaming for the things that you are unhappy or frustrated about?

Learned helplessness

Sometimes when I coach people, I discover that they find it hard to see beyond the boundaries and apparent constraints of their current situation. A kind of institutionalised reliance seems to blunt the sharp edge of initiative, experimentation and hope. In the worst cases, a kind of corporate laziness develops. Dependency converts into feeling stuck – inertia, impotency and indecision.

You can even develop characteristics much like those of children returning home from university. Even though they are perfectly capable of looking after themselves, they revert to semi-childish behaviour and expect everything to be done and provided for them. The peanut butter jar is left open on the kitchen surface, the mugs are left in the sitting room and the towels on the bathroom floor.

There is a term for this: it's called 'learned helplessness' and it has three main dimensions. You need to check whether you fall into any of these, as a habit or from time to time, because they can slow your progress and suck out your energy.

The first is *permanence*. You get stuck because you think things can't change. You feel something is going to be a certain way forever. It might be the way you think about your opportunities, your situation or your own abilities. It could be your financial situation or perhaps something to do with relationships. Now you know about it, watch out for it and catch it before it develops into a pattern that holds you back.

The second aspect is called *pervasiveness*. This indicates a type of pessimistic approach that believes that absolutely everything is going wrong or everything is badly affected by a particular situation or set of circumstances. When a problem makes you feel that everything is falling apart then you are letting *pervasiveness* interfere with your potential for success and resilience. I once found myself cursing the plumbing in my whole house because we'd had a couple of leaks, but the truth was there were just a couple of leaks. Sometimes you might say, 'I have a terrible job', or 'I hate my job/life', because of a few difficult meetings with customers.

The third aspect is *personalisation*. If, when problems occur, you become self-critical and self-disparaging, this could be one for you to look out for. If you do a bad presentation, for example, you can react by thinking, 'I am usually pretty good at presentations, but today I wasn't as energetic/clear/logical as I usually am'; or you might hear that little voice in your head saying, 'That was rubbish and I am rubbish at speaking to groups of people and I don't know why I bother'. You can see how destructive the second approach will be if you let it take hold.

You already have what you want

Someone once made this provocative statement to me: 'You already have what you want.' I immediately thought of gazillions of reasons why this couldn't possibly be true. But, as this statement bounced around in my head, the kernel of truth it contains (not my head, the statement) began to reveal itself to me. I'm sure you've already worked it out – if you *really* want it, you'll have found a way to get it. In other words you will have been really resourceful rather than helpless.

You will have focused, committed, been disciplined and had some luck. Luck, as you know, tends to come your way when you are focused, committed and disciplined. It's easy for you to explain away why you shouldn't attempt something; why there is no way it can happen. But who would have imagined we would see a double amputee running in the Olympics? You would take one look at him and say, 'No you can't do that' and you'd have been wrong.

If you think you can do a thing or think you can't do a thing, you're right

HENRY FORD

How much of what you want do you have? Have you ever really thought about what you want, or have you allowed others to fill in the blanks, only for you to find that it isn't the way you would have done it? If you'd only taken the time, put in the effort and had the courage to make work and life what you really want.

The first part of choice is checking that you haven't given up the responsibility to others; the second part is deciding what you really want. How can you work out what you really want?

Do the right thing

A series of short interviews with conventionally successful business people in a supplement of a Sunday newspaper ended with the question, 'What would you really like to have done?' You can imagine the sort of answers that the interviewer received – artist, sportsperson, musician, explorer and so on. Of more than 20 of these interviews I read, only one person answered *'This is* what I wanted to do!' Even the supposedly successful may spend a significant proportion of their lives doing something they don't want to do as much as something else they'd rather be doing. Isn't that curious?

At a TED talk in 2009, Alain de Botton spoke about how bad it is not getting what you want, but even worse to have an idea of what you want and to find out at the end of the journey that it isn't, in fact, what you wanted. This is the problem with following an idea of success that isn't really your own or that you haven't honestly considered. You can so easily aspire to the type of 'success' others appear to have, in the hope that it will give you what you want.

What makes you leap out of bed with excitement? What would send you off with a spring in your step every day?

CHOOSE | 21

Do you qualify?

Even as I write this, there is that rationalising voice in my head saying 'Ah, but we can't all be pop stars and artists and sports people.' It might be in yours as well. Where does that voice come from? My bet is that it will be someone from your formative years. Someone from your childhood possibly gave you the impression that doing something you really enjoy, gain satisfaction and fulfilment from is only for a special few – whoever they may be. I'm not sure of the qualifications. I'm not sure why you or I should disqualify ourselves.

Of course it's not a problem, actually, because there are enough people who do love to do the things that I don't love to do and enough of them who don't love to do what I love to do – which means that we can all do what we love to do. How can this be possible? Surely there must be something that has to be done which no-one would love to do – isn't there? Well, maybe love isn't always the right word. For some, a calling or a sense of vocation or duty or a belief system is the most important and motivating thing.

I know someone whose profession is insurance and he loves his job. I know someone else whose job is reinsurance – and he loves his work too! Who'd have thought?

There are a significant numbers of people who are doing exactly what they want to do, but there are many, many more who are not. Tony Robbins, the well-known motivational speaker and coach, said, 'One reason so few of us achieve what we truly want is that we never direct our focus; we never concentrate our power. Most people dabble their way through life, never deciding to master anything in particular.'

Comfortable inaction

Accepting mediocrity and accepting dissatisfaction is still more comfortable than questioning yourself about what would really give you a kick, a buzz, satisfaction, inspiration and fulfilment in the long term. It really is. You can endure it. It is easier than doing something about it.

Are you dabbling your way through your life? Are you gritting your teeth and letting too much of your potential go to waste? In fact, you've been okay with this book up to this point because the idea of re-evaluating and taking a breather all sounds very nice. You might be feeling excited now at the possibility of a personal breakthrough. You might be feeling daunted because it seems too difficult.

Whether you are feeling excited or daunted, at some point you'll have to deal with that voice which starts to say, 'Can't be done', 'Won't happen', 'Not possible', 'Who are you kidding?' Here's a suggestion: let's just put that on hold for a while. Every time it pops up, just bash it down again. In fact better than that, just ignore it. Stop thinking that way. It's okay. This creates a vacuum and you have to fill it with something. There will come a point when you will need to deal with the questions and the challenges, but not yet.

Pursue your own path

When President Kennedy announced that the USA would put a man on the moon, he didn't focus on why it couldn't be done. If you are not going to let the discouragements and conventional opinions of others get on top of you and defeat you, there has to be something which is all yours that is driving you. First, you have to fill the vacuum. First get the vision and the belief then you have a far greater chance of overcoming the obstacles and barriers to reaching that vision.

What is your purpose? Yowsers! A scary question for most. It can sound daunting or maybe even too grand and a bit too serious. So let's de-mythologise it. What does it really mean? It's your focus – your reason for getting out of bed. When you listen to people who are completely involved in what they are doing, it is often a mixture of desire, fascination, dissatisfaction and pleasure. There is always a journey involved. Realisations, steps forward, steps backward, breakthroughs and disappointments punctuate the journey. It's a voyage of discovery.

For some it is absolutely obvious from early on. I met a guy the other day who told me how much he loved computer programming because of the problem solving and challenges. He started when he was nine years old. Others trace back their passion to early dreams. Don't worry if you don't know instantly what your purpose is. Start thinking about what it might *possibly* be.

Often the seeds will be in your history. You may already be doing it, or some of it, but you haven't embraced it fully enough yet. There are probably parts of your work or business which excite you more than others. When you think about it, these things have overlaps and connections with other things you did well at school or in other jobs or maybe in your social life.

Here's a useful way to start thinking about it. If you can combine what you are passionate about with your talent, knowledge and experience and be paid the amount of money you want, you have a formula for lasting success. There are other important ingredients, but this is a good beginning.

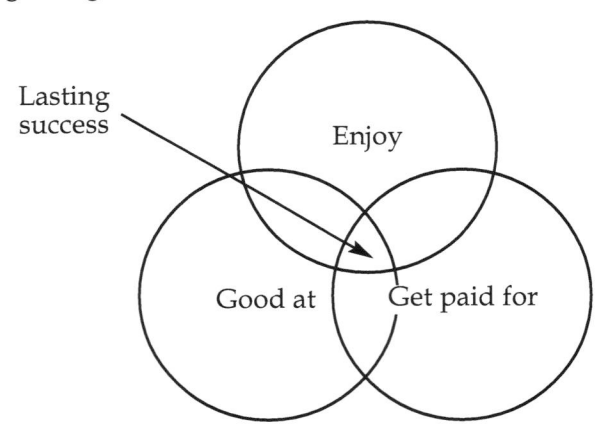

Lasting success → Enjoy / Good at / Get paid for

Invaluable exercise

Years ago, I read the classic book, *What Colour is Your Parachute?* The exercises helped me identify quite a few things that I enjoyed and that were important to me. But having identified them, it isn't easy to turn them into the perfect vocation in one huge leap. Often you have to go through a number of smaller changes and keep adjusting along the way as you keep noticing what is bringing out the best in you and helping you to fulfil your potential.

So why not give it a go? If you have never really thought about this before, now is your opportunity. Look back on your life and career so far. Why not try writing down a few things that made you feel good, that felt important, worthwhile and enriching? You could draw a timeline, if you like, and think about the times when you were happiest, most fulfilled and effective. You are not too young or too old to do this exercise.

Get off the launchpad

Believing that having the work and life you want is only for the chosen few will hold you back. That mindset is robbing you of achieving a more fulfilling and rewarding work and life. Your working life is likely to be much longer than you might have imagined, so make sure you are enjoying it as much as possible. You can have what you want if you are prepared to put in the effort. Doing what you enjoy, are good at and can be well rewarded for, is what will feel like real success. If you are not sure about what you are doing or what you find enjoyable, now is the time to blow off the cobwebs so that you can achieve more success more easily.

If this has set your brain off and running that's great, but if you are like me, and many others I have trained, it takes a bit of work to get the juices flowing. It's understandable. You were never taught to think about what you really want. In fact, you were probably positively discouraged from letting your mind wander. If when you're five years old you tell your mum that you want to be an astronaut, she'll make encouraging noises, but try that 15 years later and she'll tell you not to be so silly. Let's look at how you can develop the kind of thinking that will give you a rich and motivating vision that will energise and excite you.

BIG MENTAL NOTE

If you don't design your life someone else will do it for you and you may not like the choices they make.

| ONE SMALL STEP |

Where are you directing your focus? What will you master so that you won't dabble your way through life?

---

3 | DREAM

Unlock the might of your imagination

Imagination is more important than knowledge

ALBERT EINSTEIN

Daydream believer

You know how, when you go to a great movie or read a particularly good book, you often think 'How did they come up with that?' and wonder at the fabulous and unusual ideas. 'What an imagination that writer/director must have!'

Do you know how they do that? They use their imagination. Day after day, they come up with ideas for how to do things. They are in the business of 'being creative', so almost everything that they come across goes through the filter of their senses and their thinking and playing, and they constantly ask themselves, 'How could I use that for a story or an idea?'

Do you know what else? Most of the ideas they come up with are nonsense, just like yours. But they produce so many of them that in the end they get something good, something worth working on. Sometimes, what starts out as nonsense becomes fabulous. They experiment with bringing humour, pain, tragedy, suspense, fear and joy to life on the screen, on the page, through the dialogue, music, colour and action. They also beg, borrow, steal, copy and mash-up other things they've seen and heard before. Creativity is 90 percent perspiration and 10 percent inspiration. But you couldn't possibly do anything like that. Could you?

You are probably a pretty rational person. You have grown up in a developed world-style education system. You know how to analyse. You think a lot. You've accumulated a lot of knowledge. Good thing too. It helps with so much that you have to do well in order to live, but it's not enough. You have to dream dreams too. You have to free your mind a little bit.

My guess is that you haven't been given very much training in how to use your imagination. How many classes did you go to where they taught you how to develop a vision for yourself? At school you were probably told to *not* daydream. So it is difficult and feels unnatural for you to allow your mind to wander. If you only gave a little bit more freedom to that imaginative part of your brain, who knows what exciting sparks, thoughts and connections you'd create that would launch you into orbit?

Let your mind wander, let your mind wonder

Still not convinced? So what are you telling me: that some people (the creative ones) have little bits of brain and connections that you don't have? I don't doubt that there are people who are particularly gifted in this field, but most just haven't bothered to try. You haven't developed your potential. Have you got a fixed view of yourself including that you don't have a very good imagination? When God gave out the imaginations, was he/she scraping around in the bottom of the barrel when it came to you?

Think about it like this: your imagination is like an under-used muscle. If you have ever attempted to resume some kind of physical exercise routine after a break, you'll know that it can be quite hard work to get muscles going again. I have broken a few bones through over-boisterous participation in various sports. When the cast comes off, you have this pathetic, shrivelled excuse for a limb underneath, which needs some serious rehabilitation to get it working properly again.

The hardest part is just getting started. It is surprisingly easy to do what we want to do when we know what it is that we want.

You don't have to follow the flock

Of course, following the flock appears to be the safest option until your organisation gets delayered and you happen to be in one of the unnecessary layers. Successful people know where they want to go and what they want to achieve. They are not derailed by setbacks – even big ones.

When my 'dyed in the wool' Yorkshireman physics teacher asked a question of me in class and I paused, he'd hurry me for the answer. If I said I was thinking about it he would retort, 'Ee don't boast lad, t'sheep on my brother's farm have got more brains than thee.' Yes, he really did speak like that. Guess what this did for my confidence and to my physics results.

This clearly isn't true. Sheep don't have more brains than me! What does a sheep do? Just follows the flock. If you watch sheep for a while, one or two start moving to another part of the field and one by one the rest look up, see the others moving and think 'Oh, I had better go where they are going.' And so they do.

No imagination, see!

Imagymnation

Ok – I agree. Terrible word. But your imagination needs exercise.

People who be who they want to be and do what they want to do and get what they want to get, talk about having a dream or vision. Dreams are usually vivid, not very logical, slightly (or very) weird – and that's what makes them compelling. Dreams that come in our sleep have these characteristics and we don't have much control over them at all. But positive daydreaming is completely different and it is called exercising your imagination.

How can you put this to work? How could you start to use your imagination to help you get to where you want to go and enjoy the journey along the way? Remember, success is the journey as well as the destination. This is why for some life seems to pass them by, but never seems to arrive. When I get a boyfriend/girlfriend, I'll be happy.

When I get to the university I want to go to, I'll be happy. When I get that job/house/partner/car/children… When I get a *new* partner/house/car, I'll be happy.' You are wishing your life away instead of imagining and speaking into existence the life you want day by day.

Picture perfect

Instead, you could start to develop a vivid picture of becoming more and more what you want to be. Of course you'll have to have some ideas about this. Sportspeople have a clear idea of what success looks like for them. They visualise it. They see themselves in their mind's eye in full colour with the crowd roaring. As well as practising their physical strengthening exercises and technique, they use their minds to train their bodies to perform.

But your mind isn't used to this, so you'll have to begin to train it to develop the picture and then make it stronger. Imagine a field that hasn't been walked through. The grass is long and the ground is rough. The first day you walk through that field how much impression will you make? How about the second, or even the third? What about after a week or two? How about a month?

This is the way you form new thinking habits.

If you want to be a more energetic, determined, happy, resourceful person, start thinking about yourself that way. Give yourself a boost! Muhammad Ali said 'The man with no imagination has no wings'. Isn't this extraordinary? It isn't just about willpower or intelligence or skill or luck. It's about vividly imagining yourself as the success you want to be, as well as putting in all the effort and hard work that will get you where you want to go.

Perception and Reality

Here's something to take on board if you can. Your brain and body can't tell the difference between something you intensely imagine, and reality. The subconscious mind does not distinguish a real from an imagined experience. In life you tend to get what you repeatedly focus on.

Exercising your imagination could be the beginning of a major breakthrough for you. The possibilities are literally endless. Just look at what some people have accomplished. Why not you? Why not begin to dream some new bigger, better possibilities for yourself? When you allow yourself to dream some dreams, it could lead you to surprising and pleasant places.

Here's a warning. If you think of some possibilities and then think of all the reasons why they can't happen, your imagination will shut down again. So allow yourself some time to play with ideas without thinking about the implications or the how. If you worry about those, your logical brain will take over again and your creativity will shut down. If you let ideas flow, they tend to build on each other and you'll surprise yourself with what's inside your head and heart.

Once you start to free your mind from its analytical shackles, all sorts of ideas will begin to pop into your mind. Usually, just as you are dropping off to sleep or in the shower or walking the dog. Make sure you have a little notebook with you (okay, next to the shower) because you don't want to lose these ideas and random thoughts. Often they connect up, but not in a logical order. If you prefer, make sure you know how to put voice messages into your smartphone or save notes.

If it's meant to be it's up to me

Where would you like to be in three years time?

It's okay, I already know the answer.

You don't know where you'd like to be in three years time.

No problem. Let your imagination get to work. Most of your thinking about the future up to this point may have been in the form of worrying or stress. Many people are like that. You think about the past, the present and the very near future, not wanting to look too far ahead. Not much further than the weekend, or holiday, or Christmas. That's why shops start advertising Christmas goods earlier and earlier. They know that after you have had your summer holiday you need the next event to focus on.

Speaking of holidays, how many of us would just turn up at the airport and jump on the next plane? We give some thought to where we want to go beforehand. In fact, we probably give more thought to what we are going to have for Christmas lunch than we do about where we want to be in two, three or five years time. What is it that's stopping you from creating your own future?

Could you estimate how much of your future is dependent on you? 30 percent, 50 percent, 80 percent. Let's say that it's at least 50 percent. If you could develop a great vision for yourself and at least 50 percent of it happened in the next three years, how would that be? Pretty good, I would think. Better than now?

Or you could be like the majority of people and just trust to luck and spend most of your time thinking about what you don't want. You become what you think about most of the time. Successful people are visionary. They create a strong picture in their mind's eye and then make it a reality. They make choices, work hard and strangely lucky things happen to them along the way.

Getting started

I know people can find this tricky. Why should you be any good at it if you've never practised it much before? So, here are a few ways to get going. Set aside a few undisturbed hours. They could literally change your life.

VISION PRACTISE #1
1. Use the magic word
What's that? *Possibly*. When you start with these vision exercises, you can feel like you are committing yourself to something without knowing whether that is really what you want. Using 'possibly' allows you to explore some ideas.

2. Use a question
Imagine you are sitting by a pool in three years time, sipping your favourite drink and saying how fantastic the last three years have been.

"What could *possibly* have happened in those three years to make you feel that they have been fantastic?"

3. Use 'Freewriting'

Here's the problem. As soon as our imagination starts to answer the question, our conscious mind starts to throw up all the objections as to why what you have written is impossible. Then your imagination will dry up. What you need to do is create, but don't edit. That comes later. So try it like this…

Write for 90 seconds *without stopping*.

Don't worry about your punctuation, grammar or spelling – just write down your thoughts even if it is 'I'm not sure what to write next'. The idea is to develop a free flow of thought that will help you with the next stage. Content really isn't important at this stage. You are training your mind to learn how to be more future-oriented and visionary.

Tip: If you are using a computer cover the screen so that you can't see what you are writing.

VISION PRACTISE #2
1. Think about this in a more complete way.
Remember you are still by the pool (or somewhere else that would be a meaningful and wonderful place for you to be – hmm, that's worth imagining). Use the same technique, but apply it to all the important areas of your life.

1. "What have I achieved in my career/business in the last three years to make me feel that they have been fantastic?"
2. "What have I achieved in my personal development in the last three years to make me feel that they have been fantastic?"
3. "What have I achieved as a wife/husband/partner in the last three years to make me feel that they have been fantastic?"
4. "What have I achieved as a parent in the last three years to make me feel that they have been fantastic?"
5. "What have I achieved in my hobbies and interests in the last three years to make me feel that they have been fantastic?"
6. "What have I contributed to wider society or those less fortunate than myself?"

2. If not now, when? If not you, who?

There is no perfect time and waiting for it will put you at risk of becoming dependent, sluggish and hopeless. It gets harder and harder because you become more and more entrenched. Here are some of the excuses you might make

I can't afford to...
When I get that promotion...
I am too old to change/learn/try...
I'll do it when I retire...
It'll be easier when the kids have left home...
If only...

Dan Priestley uses a great little illustration in his book, *Key Person of Influence*. He writes that waiting for the situation to be perfect before you take action is like lying in bed waiting for all the lights to turn green before you go to work. Most people who achieve things overcome obstacles in themselves and in their circumstances. You will have already done this in some areas of your life, so remember when you did and do more of that. Don't settle for less than the best you want.

BIG MENTAL NOTE

Give a little bit more freedom to that imaginative part of your brain. Who knows what exciting sparks, thoughts and connections you'll create?

| ONE SMALL STEP |

When will you do your first Vision Practise? Choose a time and a place and tell someone else you are going to give it a go!

DREAM | 33

4 | SHINE

Enjoy your journey and look out for pitfalls

Too often we believe that enjoyment is what has to be sacrificed to the goal of excellence

TIMOTHY GALLWEY

Stay in peak condition

Getting to the top will be easier if you stay in peak condition. If you want to be successful at what you do, look after yourself. Keeping in good physical condition will help you to maintain the energy levels and prevent you being exhausted. Physical energy contributes to mental energy. If, for example, you are feeling lethargic because of lack of sleep, it is guaranteed to show up in the way you can apply your mind to the challenges and opportunities you have. Of course, there are times when a new arrival in the family, sickness or other circumstances can affect sleep patterns. That's when you need to be particularly aware and find the support you need.

If you are overweight, it affects your energy levels. Make sure you are eating a good diet. All the advice says that breakfast is the most important meal of the day. Is yours giving you the fuel to be dynamic? Be thoughtful about your alcohol intake. Arriving at your desk wrestling with a hangover may be funny the first few times, but it is going to take its toll and others will begin to notice. It will affect your relationships and the general impression you create about yourself. Keeping hydrated as you work is another simple but essential part of staying at the top of your game.

Success, of course, is more than skin deep. You'll need a lively mind too. Stretch your mind with ideas and materials that stimulate you.

Don't get in a rut by only reading, watching and listening to the same things day in day out. I know you need to rest your brain after a day full of problem-solving, but balance out the 'switch off' time with some activities that will interest and refresh you in different ways. It's amazing how sometimes completely unconnected ideas will help you in other areas of your life.

Be authentic

After a successful career working in various IT roles far too complex for me to understand, a friend of mine found himself in a role he didn't like. Now this friend isn't what you would call your normal IT guy. He's as comfortable communing with nature as he is designing a system. In his previous roles, which he had enjoyed, there was plenty of space for creativity and invention. He could find new ways to do things and work with innovative people on new projects. He enjoyed travelling to fascinating cities around the world.

All this changed when his division was outsourced to another company with a different culture, where he didn't have the history or relationships. He found himself assigned to a role with a client that involved commuting for hours on busy motorways to do a job holding very little interest or pleasure for him. As his friends, we were saddened as it seemed to literally suck the life out of him. He became unwell and less happy. Everything about that job seemed to clash with what makes him tick.

It's important to develop your picture of success in a way that enables you to genuinely express your best qualities. I've seen many people who have repressed their temperament, either because they thought that was expected or due to fear. This will make you unhappy. It's called being incongruent. It is bad for your emotional state to stifle your personality and it affects the way people perceive you. Inauthentic people tend to unwittingly radiate an atmosphere that restricts building trust with others. My friend had the courage to make the choices which means he now has the freedom to pursue his passions and interests.

Ignoring isn't bliss

Have you sometimes looked at yourself and wondered, 'What's happened to my get up and go? Where has my va va voom gone?' The problem could be that you are ignoring what is important to you. Have you lost sight of the things you enjoy doing? Have you assumed that you can enjoy life outside what you call work, but that the rest of it just has to be put up with?

The traditional zoo has gone through something of a revolution in recent years and important work is done for the conservation of wild animals, but it still saddens me to see animals that enjoy a whole jungle now living in an enclosure. It just doesn't seem right. Where are you living? Are you in *your* natural habitat or have you come to accept a lesser and limiting existence.

The signs are there. Often it's called stress, sometimes depression. For others it's a short temper and yet others have difficulty sleeping. You may have even noticed that alcohol has become your go-to solution (literally) for stress relief. In a strange way, you can easily just get used to these things. You can start to accept them as a normal part of life. It is easy to become desensitised to them. At another level it can be the feeling that you are just not being yourself and that nagging question, 'How did I end up doing this?' Maybe you are just not doing very well at your job or relationships are strained.

Out of step

If you have that feeling of being out of step with yourself, there is a good chance that you are not living or working according to your own values. This doesn't mean that everything is wrong with every part of life. You probably don't need to abandon your family, fire your boss and make for the nearest desert island, but you do need to take notice that all is not well in your world.

There are many different kinds of values which could be important to you, but you've never really identified them before and therefore you haven't realised their significance. One of the best ways to find more happiness and success in work is to be doing more of what you want to do in a way that you want to do it. Don't be put off by 'values' exercises you have done with organisations that do anything but live by them.

A very basic starting point for most would be that what you do is honest and legal, not simply in a criminal sense but according to the regulations of your industry. Not everywhere you work will be operating in that way and it could be important for you to question it. At another level, perhaps creative freedom or the room to show high levels of initiative are important to you. In one job I felt very constrained by my boss and, despite a number of changes, I just couldn't feel comfortable in the role. When I discussed this with him he said, 'I have never given anyone as much freedom as I have given you.' Neither of us was wrong, we just had differing values and expectations.

This left me with a choice. I could negotiate more freedom, but that would mean that I would probably have to take his job at some point. I could stay and accept the level of initiative and decision-making. I could stay and complain about my boss – or I could decide to take the next steps in my journey. So that's what I did.

When you acknowledge there is a problem, it's comforting to know that there is a really good reason for it. There is something in your world which is out of keeping with your inner world – who you are really. It isn't so much about what you are doing, although it could be, but the way that you are doing it or the values of the people or organisation you're with.

Don't get discouraged. There is a solution. Whether you only need to make a few personal adjustments in terms of personal attitude, or you need to find a different job, take it one step at a time.

Use it or lose it

The wonderful thing about working out some values is that they act as guiding principles as you pursue your purpose and realise your vision by acting on your goals. These are the principles that, when lived by, will make you feel alright with the world and with yourself. Listening to yourself, being aware of what's working and isn't working, can genuinely guide you. And life is much easier with a guide. Trouble is, if you keep ignoring your guide it will give up and go away and you won't be able to hear it any more. Doing this will make you more unhappy.

I was speaking with a client who was considering a move from his current position. We started to work out what was important for him. He noted things like integrity, working in a team that really is a team and people living according to their stated values. Earlier in the year he'd experienced a good deal of unhappiness and anger because he'd encountered some behaviour in colleagues that flew in the face of these things. Should he just carry on and hope it would go away, as it sometimes does, or would he need to take action himself?

No, there isn't a happy ending. He decided to stay despite the fact that a number of things important to him and affecting his quality of life were consistently undermined. Why would he do this? A whole number of reasons, but one of the main ones is fear. The result is you're deferring your happiness and greater success until that golden day when you retire and then you can have the life you want. Why not work for it now, instead of 10, 20 or 30 years from now.

Avoid the dark side

To the casual observer, he had it all: film star good looks, beautiful wife, a very long and successful professional career and, as the manager, he'd even helped the Welsh football team achieve some success. But in November 2011, at only 42, Gary Speed committed suicide. What was most startling to me about this sad story was how, one by one, his closest friends and people he'd known the longest confessed they had no idea that he was in the state of mind that caused him to take his own life.

Over the following months a number of prominent sports people, mostly men as I recall, appeared on several radio and television programmes to speak about their own battles. Some have written about it in their autobiographies. Surprising figures like Neil Lennon, a Glaswegian footballer with a hard man image; Freddie Flintoff, the apparently happy go lucky England cricketer; and others such as Stephen Fry have spoken of their experiences of depression in varying degrees.

It seemed that at last it was okay to talk about depression without too much shame. Ask the relevant professionals and they will tell you that there are all sorts of different kinds of depression and of course there's a long list of complicated names and definitions which classify them. They'll also tell you that one in 10 people experience some kind of depression. I suspect it could be much higher.

Stress factors

I am not clinically trained, but different phases of my career have brought me into contact with a lot of people at a personal as well as a professional level. Having been a pastor in a large city church and now working with high achieving business people, the conversations and insights I have had into the lives of those I have worked with have often been very open and honest. I am writing in this section from a non-medical professional point of view.

What I see is that people firstly don't really notice what is going on, even with themselves. In the world of business you may talk about feeling stressed a lot and it is part of the accepted experience of work and business. You may even acknowledge there is good stress and bad stress. There are times when you will be stressed, maybe even very stressed, but you know it's okay. In fact you are cracking on, rather than cracking up.

Then there are other times when you need to notice that something different is happening. There are different signs with different people. Loss of appetite, difficulty sleeping, lack of motivation, not wanting to be bothered, feelings of isolation, thoughts of hopelessness and not being able to cope. You may notice that your relationships are being affected.

Never give in

Reading this book, you may imagine me as a naturally positive, outgoing and optimistic person; someone with a fair amount of drive, a positive self-image and someone who enjoys a challenge and wants to achieve. You'd be right. I am like that, but sometimes I battle with negative thoughts about my situation, my future and myself.

Occasionally that negativity gets very strong and I can feel even a degree of hopelessness creeping over me.

Quite a while ago I experienced what I preferred to call burnout. It was a seriously low time. It continued for a number of months. I never went to a doctor because I didn't want anything like that on my medical records; anyway, I was determined to beat it through sheer willpower and I was definitely not going to use medication. At times I wondered if I could carry on.

One day I picked up a book: it told a story of how Winston Churchill closed a speech at Harrow School with the words, 'Never give in. Never give in. Never, never, never, never – in nothing, great or small, large or petty – never give in.' Those words, and the enduring love and commitment of my fabulous wife, family and friends got me through.

So I thought I'd beaten it; I had toughed it out. Then a few years ago my wife said to me one day, 'Do you think you suffer from depression?' Having resisted the thought because 'I am not that sort of person', I realised that she could be right. My periods of lowness, low motivation and feeling demoralised, even if not as extreme as previously, were still getting to me and stopping me from enjoying life and achieving my goals. From that point on I have taken my 'mood' much more seriously and found all sorts of reliable strategies for lifting it. I write this because of the tendency there is for you to ignore it.

Danger signs

I've worked out the warning signs for me that things are not okay. In some ways I can't tell you the reasons, but I can see the signs and the times. The strange thing about the changes in my mood is that they often don't appear to be logical. Life and work can all be fine and dandy, but the clouds may still roll in.

Some of my warning signs are:

- Over-stressed when driving
- Picky and critical with others
- Lacking motivation
- Deeply pessimistic

I also know when my vulnerable times are:

- Just before, during and just after holidays
- When I have an illness and after an illness
- When I have an injury and after an injury (sporting)
- When I feel I have done a lot for others with little return

I have worked out my own ways of keeping the clouds away without using medication of a legal or other kind, and without resorting to over consumption of any beverages. I am not giving advice to you here, for obvious reasons, except to say, if this is you, to whatever degree and however often, don't just cope. Be open with someone you trust and find some solutions. You'll be a lot happier and you'll recover your get up and go. Today could be the first day of the rest of your life. Today could be your turning point.

Success doesn't often get dished up on a plate. It takes dedication, commitment and all round personal awareness to bring out the best in you and those around you. Condition yourself as a whole person if you are in it for the long run. Be resilient, but at the same time admit your weaknesses and work out how to manage them. It also takes huge amounts of self-belief, action and motivation and that's where we are going next.

BIG MENTAL NOTE

One of the best ways to find more happiness and success in work is to do more of what you want to do in a way that you want to do it.

| ONE SMALL STEP |

Write down five values that are important to you and score out of five how well your work matches them? (e.g. Caring, Fun, Honesty, Intellectual challenge, Self-development)

5 | FOCUS

Make action plans not wish lists

No one ever got to the top of Mount Everest just by wandering about.

ZIG ZIGLAR

Nothing but a dreamer

The problem with all this vision, values and imagination malarkey is that you could end up with your head in the clouds. So heavenly-minded that you are no earthly good. 'All mouth and no trousers,' as my dad used to say. And the problem with just wandering about is you could end up anywhere. A dead-end, for example, or a job you don't like or do as wholeheartedly as you could.

Some friends and I decided to replicate a charity bike ride we had completed the previous year. As it was a long, off-road ride, it was a complicated route through forests, fields, gullies, tracks and rough ground of many types – not many roads. Now the great thing about a charity bike ride is that it tends to be pretty well organised. The route is signposted, stewards make sure you go in the right direction and there are checkpoints along the way where you can refuel and regroup. We soon discovered that nine mates with a very small map and nine different opinions is a very different proposition leading to hilarious consequences.

We started off from the same point as the previous year, a university, and quickly realised that we didn't even know how to get off the campus. After riding around aimlessly for a few minutes, someone confidently led off – only to take us into a car park completely enclosed by tall buildings on three sides. Twelve hours and many wrong turns later, we had completed an 80-mile journey and only seven of us made it all the way. It had taken us just eight hours the year before.

Get into goals

You must have a direction and you need a plan of how you'll get from A to B. How are you going to progress from where you are to where you want to be? Although a well-organised bike ride sounds very appealing, life isn't often like that. There isn't a clearly signposted route and B isn't necessarily precisely defined. You have to create your own plan otherwise you risk losing your way, and achieving your purpose could take much longer. You have to make your best guess at what B looks like. It's a little bit like thinking first what country or region you want to go to on holiday rather than knowing exactly which hotel.

Don't put off working on your goals because you are not absolutely clear about the details of each step. The important thing is to get moving. If you wait until you have the perfect plan, you won't get the momentum that you need to make the changes in your life that you want.

If you do find yourself constantly questioning and hesitating, it's called the paralysis of analysis. I am not suggesting that you simply impulsively change direction and make blind decisions. Make informed choices, but be brave as well. Otherwise all the work you have done up to this point is wasted. There comes a time that you decide you have done enough thinking and research and it is time to come up with a plan. You can easily adjust it along the way.

Pinpoint what you will do

You may be theoretically convinced by the need for goals, but find it hard for a variety of reasons to commit yourself to making specific plans. I'd be surprised if you haven't heard about the importance of goal-setting, but neither would I be surprised if you're not in the habit of doing it. Knowing and doing are two different things. I remember abandoning a book once because it started talking about the need to set goals. I thought 'I know all about that', but the reason for my strong reaction was I didn't want to do it. I didn't want to commit myself. As we have seen, making choices is all part of taking responsibility for your own direction and progress rather than waiting to see what will happen.

The most powerful goals are the ones that come from you for you. Effective goals are written using the acronym SMART. This stands for, Specific, Measureable, Achievable, Relevant and Timed. This could be one of the things that's holding you back. It's quite hard answering these questions. I've seen all sorts of people struggle with it. How could you make it easier? One of the most helpful pieces of advice I ever read concerned the idea of prototyping, which we'll return to later, but in simple terms it means 'just have a go'.

Earlier, you thought about where you want to be in three years time in a number of areas of your life. Now it is time to start thinking how to get there. It's hard to plan it all out. The best way to start is to break it down into short, medium and long-term goals. Choose one area and set yourself a short-term goal. This has to be something you can do and have control over. For example you may want to be promoted to senior manager in 18 months time, but you don't actually control that. It is someone else's decision. That is called an *outcome* goal.

What's in your control? Your performance is in your control, so set yourself a *performance* goal that will help you get that result. Your performance goal may have something to do with getting some more training or qualifications. Then check that it is SMART.

'Complete senior managers' training programme before the end of this year' is a SMART goal.

Remember, it doesn't have to be perfect: it has to be useful and motivating. This gives you focus. You are not writing a wish list, you are writing an action plan and an action plan will bring you more success. Your goals still need to be acted upon and you will read more about that in Chapter 11.

The business of goals

Just in case your working situation is causing you to suffer from goal overload or apathy, consider this.

One enlightened manager I worked with decided to experiment during the annual round of goal-setting. Instead of calling in each of her team and giving them their performance objectives for the year ahead, she spoke to them in advance and asked them to decide their own goals and bring them to the meeting. To her great surprise, the goals the team members set for themselves were more challenging than the ones she had been going to set them.

Some people are great at setting their own goals and others don't quite function in the same way. I am surprised by the reliance I see in people who expect the boss to tell them what and how to do, even quite senior people. If you don't have your own goals, it will hold you back. You also run the risk of turning into a passenger. But, I hear you say, I am always being told what to do and what to achieve. Okay, two points.

1. If you are given goals, it is for you to negotiate and improve them so you can own them.
2. More importantly, generate your own goals and initiatives and hassle your boss with your great ideas.

You can educate your boss to back off a bit (if you need to) simply by taking initiative and responsibility. You train others how to treat you.

Show some enterprise and create your own goals. I promise you your boss will welcome this, or at least come to terms with it. No, I know I don't know *your* boss. I know they emerged from some dark, evil fissure in the earth and therefore you have every excuse imaginable not to apply this. But just in case your boss isn't evil personified, there will be a way of communicating with them which will enable you to be more self-directed and therefore more motivated.

Bad company harms good goals

Most people who achieve their goals and become successful in their chosen field surround themselves with other success-orientated people who help them foster a positive outlook. If you like, they take care of their mental environment. Let's call it *environmental awareness*.

Your mental environment is made up of three elements. Your interactions with other people (real and digital), your own self-talk, and what you consume, i.e. books, websites, TV, music, radio, video etc.

Just as we all need to care for the environment if the planet is going to continue to sustain us, you need to care for your personal mental environment if you are going to fulfil your goals. In fact you have to be aware of how each of the three elements is helping or hindering your success.

At a party one Christmas, I was in conversation with a number of other men whom I didn't know particularly well. I'd met them at similar gatherings and this time the conversation worked its way around to my 'line of work' and the fact that I was writing a book. When I described the general nature of the contents, I used the phrase *self-belief* and one of them said, 'I didn't know the British went in for that sort of thing'. I laughed it off and took a slightly larger glug of wine, while inwardly screaming, 'What the hell do you mean?' Maybe this is why the English football team always lose the penalty shoot out.

You will have to think about which friends and colleagues you spend time with because, if you are trying to get somewhere and do something with your life, you will find there are some people who'll suck the lifeblood out of you and others who will encourage you. Is it easier to just fit in and moan and complain with the rest of them? Yes. Is this going to help you achieve the quality of life and work you want? No. Guess which people it is best to spend your time with? Guess which websites it is better to visit and programmes to watch?

Does this mean you might have to spend less time with certain people? Does this mean you may risk offending some? Yes, to both. No one is negative all the time and no one is positive all the time, but you will quickly work out who it is best to be around the most. The journey to becoming more fulfilled, happy and successful isn't easy. It is tiring and challenging. This means you have to take care of yourself. One of the ways you have to take care of yourself is by being aware of the affect others have on you.

They are out to get you

Whatever you do, don't watch, listen to or read the news because this is guaranteed to fill you with a sense of powerlessness, worry and despair. Have you noticed after you have watched the news you tend to have conversations about a mysterious group known darkly as 'they'? *They* have decided to make all children under three years old do maths G.C.S.E. *They* are going to introduce police dogs with guns. If *they* are in control, what hope do you really have?

Recently I had to have a mole removed (from my neck, not the lawn). I was relieved to discover that it was not malignant, but still had to go and have advice from the nurse. She asked me if I spent very much time in the sun. Silly question – I live in England. She asked if I spent a lot of time outside. 'Only mountain biking, really', I said. 'What you have to remember is the sun is still shining even on cloudy days,' she told me. Of course I realise this, but her point was that it was still affecting my skin even though I didn't notice it.

The general background conversation in your life can often have a negative tone and it isn't good for you, especially if you are trying to change your life and fulfil even more of your potential. The great news is that you don't have to put up with it. You can change the channel, read a different section, or walk away from the conversation. Just say you have to clear some emails! You can excuse yourself from any situation if you say that.

Get out of your own way

There is one person it is difficult to get away from. That's you! Whether you like it or not, you are stuck with you and that's easier for some than others. The great thing about you is that you are always there for you. But sometimes this is not so great. In fact *a lot* of the time it's not such a great thing. How come? It's all to do with how you think and talk to yourself about yourself and your situation, simply known as self-talk.

So what is it like in your head? Is it a good place for you to be?

You've built up a picture of yourself, your reactions, capabilities and limitations, your likes and dislikes and your skills. You've gathered them over the years from your education, experiences and people who've influenced you, like your parents, peers, teachers and bosses. This can become like a set of hard and fast rules that define the parameters of your existence and are often referred to as self-beliefs.

When self-beliefs are empowering and supportive of your ambitions, they form a platform for happiness and fulfilment. If the messages you've absorbed or constructed for yourself are critical and discouraging, they become barriers to your success. Usually they're known as limiting self-beliefs, but perhaps they should be called self un-beliefs. These are the conclusions that you have drawn from your experiences.

It is impossible for you to rationally decide what to do and how to live based on all the information available. There's just too much. So you construct shortcuts and filters through which everything passes and they become the way you look at yourself, your life and the things that come your way. They are like little computer programmes running in the background. Some of them are useful and some of them are less so. It's important to identify the ones that could be slowing you down and interfering with your progress and fulfilment.

Do you have self un-belief?

You can't walk out on a conversation with yourself because, just like your shadow, you are always going to be there. The conversations you have with yourself are even more important than the conversations you have with others, so you'd better make them good ones. Why not learn to make them useful. Sometimes positive thinking and positive self-talk get a bad name. The literati tend to rubbish it. Would you rather indulge in negative thinking and negative self-talk?

Don't spend all that time developing your purpose and vision and goals only to sabotage your progress by telling yourself you are not up to it, not worth it or that you'll mess it up. I have coached many managers and leaders who fear that one day they will be found out. Even those who've attained a level of success still have to deal with that inner voice that tries to undermine them, often on a daily basis. I worked with an M.D. in an engineering consultancy, hardly the usual place for touchy feely conversations. He confessed his self-doubt about his ability to maintain his performance in the role.

Act anyway

Beliefs are what you hear when all the other voices go quiet. You can change your beliefs. Once you change your beliefs to those that support a positive self-image, your self-confidence will grow. When your self-confidence grows, you will be more assured about your purpose, goals and values. However, it would be a mistake to sit around waiting to feel good all the time before you work on and get on with your goals. I see it work both ways. People with apparently low self-esteem work hard anyway and produce great things and I've seen people with lots of self-confidence achieve little.

Work on your beliefs and, at the same, time start to write and achieve the goals you have set yourself. Achieving your goals will give you more confidence and make your view of yourself more positive. Actions make your beliefs concrete. If you are stuck – act! The next chapter gives you the secrets for finding the durable energy, passion and excitement to get what you want.

BIG MENTAL NOTE

Don't put off working on your goals because you are not absolutely clear about the details of each step. The important thing is to get moving.

| ONE SMALL STEP |

Change your self-talk to language that will turbo-charge your goals. Match it with action.

6 | ZIP

Get mountains of motivation

Your level of self-esteem, how much you like and respect yourself, is central to your levels of motivation and persistence. You should talk to yourself positively all the time to boost your self-esteem.

BRIAN TRACY

Create a new ending

You can't create a new beginning, but you can create a new ending. Your past is not the limit of your future and neither is your present. It doesn't matter which school or university you did or didn't go to; what jobs you have or haven't had. It doesn't matter how old you are or what is wrong with you. There is a whole world of opportunity for you to explore and enjoy.

It is easy for us to find every reason under the sun why others have been more successful than us. It is a great excuse for not taking any action. When you believe others have achieved what they have because they somehow have an unfair advantage, you won't have to make any demands on yourself.

George Bernard Shaw wrote that he didn't believe in circumstances because they can be an excuse. He reckoned that the people who get ahead are the people who look for the circumstances they want and if they can't find them they create them. You can be a victim of circumstances or choose not to be. Instead of blaming your situation for what you have or do not have, and what you can or cannot achieve, take full responsibility for your life, your work and your circumstances.

You could, on the other hand, start believing that you have a multitude of opportunities and you can achieve anything that you really want to. You don't have to believe it to silly extremes like 'Does that mean I can be an astronaut?' You could just believe it to the extent that you could change your career, get that promotion, increase your salary or find your soul mate and that would make a big difference to your life.

Get back on the bike

If things have been hard because you've missed an opportunity or lost a job or feel like your career is not going where you want it to, decide to change your perspective from now on. When you learn to ride a bicycle you will fall off at some point. Falling off is part of the process for learning how to stay on. This is when you have to choose whether you are going to persevere or not. As all parents know, you tell your child to get back on the bike. Still hurting, still bruised and scratched, you get back on the bike. Even if your past has been particularly tough, learn the lessons and move on.

I am writing this following Britain's Olympic and Paralympic year. One of the most extraordinary stories is about a paralympic athlete who never even made it to the games because when he was training for his event he was hit by a van driven by a drunk driver hurling him into the air. He was severely injured and left with even less mobility than he already had. When he was interviewed later, all he could talk about was how he would now have to modify his equipment and technique and what he would now do to train and carry on competing, despite his new injuries and restrictions. Wow!

Set yourself free from your past. It's not as if you can change it. This could be the most important point for you in this whole book. I have had a less than conventional career. I have reached different points in my life when I have felt severely disadvantaged by this, so much so that at times I have not known which way to turn. I clearly remember sitting in my study as a newly self-employed consultant with an empty diary, a silent telephone and an almost non-existent network of contacts.

As I was searching my brain and my books and articles for some help, I read this statement from the chief executive of a company that was going through hard times. He said, 'You have to play the cards you've been dealt.' It was the key that helped me unlock the next stage.

I used to play card games regularly as I was growing up and sometimes you get a terrible hand; it is amazing, though, how many hands you can win if you play those cards as best you can. So that's the attitude I adopted. One old contact came to mind who I hadn't spoken to for at least 10 years and, as a result of reconnecting, I did tens of thousands of business with people he introduced me to in his company. Of course this also required a lot of effort and perseverance.

Grab life by the throat

Accept right now that what you do with your life from this day forward is up to you. You can take life by the throat and do your absolute best to discover and fulfil what you are here for. What's your contribution? You can follow your interests until they turn into passions. You can allow your curiosity to lead you to your destiny. You can look into your history and see the sparks that can grow into big blazing fires.

Just this morning I spoke to someone who said he wished it were Friday every day. I'm not sure if he really meant it or whether he thought that this is what he was supposed to say. Work is out of fashion. It's much easier to say how much you hate it and how difficult it is, rather than say you love it. It becomes a self-fulfilling prophecy. For many it's seen as the thing that gets in the way of leisure and relaxation, as if they were the sole reason and purpose for living. The people to be envied most are those who are working at something they enjoy and is worthy of their talents and time.

Mighty motivation

It is almost impossible to be highly motivated about something you don't enjoy or find fulfilling on a number of levels. Getting what you want by doing exactly what you enjoy is not the natural state of things, otherwise everybody would be doing it. To get from where you are to where you want to be, you'll need to build up masses of motivation. You can kind of get by on little bits of motivation – you'll have little spurts of energy – but the people who really do something create an absolute lake of motivation. Have you wondered why you get temporarily invigorated and inspired only for it to peter out?

The answer's simple: you haven't got enough motivation. It's not strong or powerful enough or clear enough.

In earlier years of the EU, journalists would report on butter mountains and milk lakes because of an overproduction of dairy products due to subsidies. Well that's what you need now: mountains of motivation. A massive butter mountain of motivation. Imagine it – a great big yellow motivation monster that thunders along destroying every obstacle in its path. Get carried away.

What if you had more motivation than you needed? What if you overproduced motivation? Wouldn't that be fantastic? You'd be unstoppable! Making excuses and giving up would truly be a thing of the past. How would that feel?

More than a feeling

I believe motivation is a feeling. Why do I believe that? Because I know the difference in how I feel when I am revved up and ready to go and just dying to write, for instance, and when I am not. You know that feeling too. Even if it is in your dim and distant past, even back to your childhood, it's there. If it just pops up now and again, think about when you get it. How would it be if, instead of groaning every morning, you couldn't wait to get out of bed? So how do you get and keep the feeling?

Try looking at it this way. Motivation has two parts, *away from* motivation and *must have* motivation.

How do you get *away from* motivation? Think of all the things that you are absolutely tired of putting up with. What is really hacking you off? What *must not* stay this way? Often when I ask people what they want to do, they don't know, but ask them what they don't want to do and they can tell you immediately. This is *away from* motivation and you need it. Often it will be what gets you out of a bad place or apathy and inertia, but it's not enough.

It could be that you are tired of not having enough money or enough time for the other things in life that excite you. You may be totally frustrated that your life is being dominated by work that doesn't reward or fulfil you. You could be thoroughly sick of driving around in that old heap of a car. Perhaps you're mad about living in a house that's too small for you and your family. What have you had enough of? Whatever it is, feel it. Feel dissatisfied. Feel angry. Feel bad – really bad. Don't ignore it. This is your *away* motivation and it needs to be strong. Don't stand for it any more!

You need a mountain of *away* motivation.

Peak conditioning!
You can get some momentum on *away* motivation, but it won't get you far enough. It is possible to stay here, but it will not get you where you need to go. It will give you the motivation to start, but not to keep going. You'll eventually become a bit like the Tasmanian devil. Just very, very angry and whirling around in circles. You have to work on part two as well.

How do you grow *must have* motivation until it is huge, like a great big unstoppable mountain of motivation? Build up a treasure chest of emotional reasons why you want things to change. This goes together with Chapters Two through to Four. Understand your purpose, activate your imagination, build your vision and develop some goals.

Now ask yourself, When I achieve my goals…

- How will it make me feel about myself each day?
- How will it affect my enjoyment of life?
- What will it give me that I've always longed for?
- Who will it help?
- What difference will it make to my loved ones?
- How will it improve my work/business?
- What will I be able to do that I can't do now?
- What will I be proud of?

When you get affected by the past it is because you bring it into the present with all the vivid memories and emotions. So now use the same power, but imagine the future and bring it into the present with all the vividness and emotion you can. Do it every day. The actor Simon Callow says that if someone says they really want to be an actor he tells them it is not enough, because you have to *need* it not just want it. He says the challenges, the rejection and the loneliness can be so overwhelming that unless you *need* it, you shouldn't do it. What do you really need?

Do it everyday

If you do it every day, you'll get it. If you don't, you won't. I wonder how often you clean your teeth? Once a day? Twice? Why do you do this? How did it come about? Probably if there is one question that every parent asks their growing children everyday, it's, 'Have you cleaned your teeth?' It doesn't matter what else is going on – this one activity takes priority. Rain or shine; school day or holiday; in sickness and in health: clean your teeth!

Now you must begin to obsess about your ambition, your desire, your success everyday, and the motivation will stay.

Chapter One asked what unconscious habits you have which are holding you back. Now it is time to develop the habits that will boost you to the next level, the next level of success, enjoyment and achievement. You know it doesn't happen by accident and it isn't down to luck. Although it is strange how much luckier you get when you know what you really want to achieve. Just like Benjamin Franklin said, 'Diligence is the mother of good luck'.

Do it every day! Deliberately condition yourself: body, mind and motivation. Dream your dream, write your goals, look after yourself and get mountains of motivation. Why stay on the launch pad when you could be in orbit?

> **BIG MENTAL NOTE**
>
> *You could start believing that you have a multitude of opportunities and you can achieve anything you really want to.*
>
> **| ONE SMALL STEP |**
>
> *Develop a daily routine to build your motivation to epic levels.*

STOP - GROW - FLOW | Chart (1)

PART ONE

Chapters 1- 6

Review each chapter and make a quick note of a thought or page number under each heading. Don't write too much. The trick is fewer notes but more action.

STOP (What do you need to stop doing?)

1.
2.
3.
4.
5.
6.

GROW (What new ways of doing things do you want to begin and how?)

1.
2.
3.
4.
5.
6.

FLOW (These are your ideas for making good practices a life-long habit)

1.

2.

3.

4.

5.

6.

PART 2

PEP

BOOST! Your Relationships

7 | ADAPT

Listening makes life easy

The World exists not merely in itself,
but *also as it appears to me.*

CARL JUNG

Pressure to persuade

Why is it that some of the brightest stars fade? How come some of those with the greatest potential don't hit the heights you expect?

A few years ago, in a leadership development programme, I was working with the senior team of a large pharmaceuticals company and I came across a guy called... well let's call him Marco. Marco was a very bright guy. You know, the type you meet who seems to have a distinct advantage over you in the brains department.

The problem for Marco, and those working with him, was that he felt compelled to use all his outstanding faculties on every occasion and as soon as he could. If people disagreed with him he found it disconcerting and it would often make him angry. He had a sort of shoot-first-ask-questions-later approach, except he never got around to the questions.

This was a pressure for Marco. He felt that he had to perform at every meeting and became stressed through worrying that he might not continually come up to the mark or make the right impression. His anxiety showed especially if anyone disagreed with him or spoilt 'the Marco show'.

Marco's pressure was matched by the frustration felt by others whenever they worked with him. For those around him it meant that discussion often turned into contention and a difficult atmosphere impeded further progress. They felt their talents and opinions were undervalued and often ignored. It meant that Marco, who was a very likeable person, was tricky to work with and when people weren't resenting his dominance they were tempted to be too dependent on him. Even more importantly, he was also struggling with negotiations with clients on contracts worth millions.

Make it easy on yourself

For Marco it was important for his wellbeing, his relationships and his prospects that he learned a better way. To progress to the level he was capable of reaching, he needed an approach that enabled him to adapt to others and attract their enthusiasm and engagement.

If there is an easier and more effective way of doing things, it would be good to know wouldn't it? Whatever business or enterprise you are involved in, you will need to achieve things by working with others. That's how things get done. So learning the important skills for getting things done with others is key to being great at work. It's key to making work less stressful and more fulfilling. Why do it the hard way if there is a smarter, quicker and easier way?

This is one of my main motivations for writing this book. After more than 12 years of coaching, training and consulting in businesses and organisations of all types and sizes, I have noticed how difficult you can make life for yourself. How? You don't habitually, easily and unconsciously use a critical set of easily-learned methods for interrelating successfully with others.

Here's number one. Learn how to use listening to make your life easier.

Listening is power

Marco had to develop a plan and some new habits; some new ways of conducting himself which, instead of focusing solely on his own brilliance, would bring out the best in everyone. Most people like the sound of an idea if it is their own. They are far more likely to respond favourably if they feel they have been listened to – if their ideas have been considered even if they are not fully adopted.

At a fundamental level, you need to learn to listen carefully to what is being asked of you. If your boss asks you to do something, make sure you check that you have understood what is required. Don't assume you know unless it is something that you've done right before. Many of the instructions and requests you will get will come via email, so you have to use a different type of 'listening.'

Frequently, emails are not written well. Subject lines are left blank or are unclear. What is required is not well-defined and deadlines aren't mentioned. People who write emails like that don't deserve to have stuff done in the way they wish or by when they want it. But you are not here to complain about them. You are here so you can have a more fulfilled and more successful life. So you know what the answer is: you have to take responsibility.

Imagine if the person making the request was a customer of yours who'd pay you money on successful completion of the task. Would you make sure you knew exactly what was required, by when? Yes, you would because that's when you'd get paid. Treat requests from your significant internal customers in exactly the same way.

The sound of silence

The first key to listening is to understand the power of your own silence. You may begin to notice that many successful people don't say very much when they're first in a conversation or meeting. Why? Because they have understood you must listen before you know what to say. Resolve to resist the temptation to be the first one to speak, especially before you know how and what others want or think. Skilled communication begins with silence, not talking. This is not an excuse for passivity or laziness.

Gaining the co-operation of others, making decisions and coming to an agreement on a way forward, can all be made much easier if you think through good questions in advance. You may be worried that if you don't get in your point first, others may gain the upper hand. Don't worry. Asking good, relevant questions puts you in control of any conversation. It will allow you to hear the point of view of others so you know how to position your own views. If knowledge is power, you'll need to listen to get the knowledge. Make sure you listen carefully to the answers. Repeat back to the other person your understanding of what they've said. Don't assume you know what they mean. Make the effort to really appreciate what they are saying before you reply.

Listening well will make life a lot easier for you. You'll appear to be the person who is intelligently evaluating the situation. You'll appear to be the person who is bringing in others' views rather than just arguing for your own. You don't have all the answers and you don't have to have them all. You can stop over-focusing on your own performance and listen to others. You can reduce the pressure to drive people along.

The best questions begin with What, Who, When, How and Where, because these are the ones that prompt others to share their opinions and ideas. This gives you the opportunity to position your views while taking their perspective into consideration. It is generally easier to reach agreement by taking this approach. You will appear constructive, helpful and wise. But there's more to it than that.

One size doesn't fit all

Have you ever wondered why you seem to connect so well with some people and yet sometimes, despite lots of apparent similarities, you don't have that same connection with others?

With some people conversations flow easily and yet with others you have to really work at it or, worse still, you really rub each other up the wrong way. Is it you or is it them? Think about colleagues and customers you interact with regularly. Are there a few with whom it would be useful if things went just a bit smoother?

Here's the thing. People tend to see the world in different ways. You may like to think that there is one objective way of looking at things (the same as yours, of course), but it simply isn't the case. This means that the way you approach a project may not be the same as Jane. The way you think about a problem is different to Dave's take on things. What is important for you in a deal won't be the same as it is for Sam. One approach doesn't suit everyone.

Why do you have a different take on the world? Here are two important ideas to consider: *nurture* and *nature*. Nurture, in this context, is all about your background, education, culture, parents' views, class and other factors that influence you.

The way you approach life is also affected by the way you tick, your nature, who you are, sometimes called your behavioural preferences. There are quite a few models out there that help you to assess yourself; you may have come across a few already. Of course everybody has their favourite so I am going to give you a mash up of a few which will give you a very practical perspective that you can use easily for some powerful results.

The best place to start is to work out what *you* are like before thinking about others and how to use your knowledge.

Personality styles - a quick guide

I am going to introduce you to four basic types. Please take on board that these are building blocks to help your understanding and, most importantly, your practical application of some introductory ideas. It's not a definitive guide to personality types. I am sure there'd be plenty of people who'd take me to task if I did make such a claim.

What I've noticed is that, unless you become a bit of a geek about such things and use them regularly, you are not going to remember abstract concepts or labels, much less use them successfully. It's considerably better to have a practical approach you can use easily every day.

Primary differences

For ease of use, I will introduce you to four styles and use a simple colours model: Red, Yellow, Blue and Green.

A Red style tends to be: results-driven, focused, task-orientated, strategic, fast-paced and may be impatient and demanding.

A **Yellow style** tends to be: sociable, fun, talkative, thinks big, a good speaker, active, may be easily distracted and may not finish tasks.

A **Blue style** tends to be: detailed, logical, systematic, analytical, thorough, and may be reserved and critical.

A **Green style** tends to be: a good listener, a team player, encouraging, thoughtful, considerate and may be stubborn and indecisive.

It's likely that you see aspects of your own style mostly in two of the colours, as this is most common. Blue/Yellow and Red/Green combinations are unusual, but everything else goes.

Understanding others

You can use the same checklist to help you to identify the style of people you know. Here are a few potential clues and indicators:

Red style: tend to speak quickly and forcefully and like you to get to the point. They are decisive and prefer to be in control. They are mostly task rather than people focused.

Yellow style: active, outgoing and spontaneous. They usually have lots going on in their lives and can be full of ideas. They don't do routine, preferring a more flexible approach to life.

Blue style: usually self-contained people, probably dress fairly conservatively, speak more slowly than the Red and Yellow style. They like routine and time to think about decisions.

Green style: general approach is laid back and relaxed. They value close relationships and tend to dress informally. Their workspace can reflect this and you may see photographs of friends and family.

No one has only the characteristics of one style. Whatever you do, don't be too simplistic and put people in just one box. In fact, everyone has all the styles to some degree, but everyone has stronger inclinations to which they automatically revert. You may see different characteristics exhibited at different times, depending on the circumstances, but when you think about it you can see what their 'normal' style is.

Use this short exercise to work out the personality style of some well-known people. Draw a box with four equal square compartments and label them for the four colours. Think of historic figures, politicians or celebrities and look at the descriptions above and start writing their names in the boxes. It's just practice.

Red	Blue
Yellow	Green

You can't really know what these people are like, but you can experiment with the ideas. You may want to put some names overlapping the edges of the border between compartments. Some may be right in the middle or others may be toward other colours. Where would you place Barack Obama? You're just taking a guess!

Mix and match

This is where the fun starts. How about trying to identify the personality style of people who are significant in your life and work? Consider five or six people who it is important for you to communicate and interact with well. It could be an important client, a fellow team member or your boss. Include one or two who are important, but you don't always connect with as well as you'd like or need to. Now use the same diagram as before, but first place your own name in the appropriate position.

Fill in the names as best you can, then you'll have a picture of where you sit in comparison to other people. One rule of thumb, as we've seen elsewhere, is that you will tend to connect well with people who are similar to you. It's the old 'birds of a feather flock together' idea. Another rule of thumb is that the people you are 'opposite' to you in style will be the least easy to connect with.

This means that Red should work well with Red, Yellow with Yellow, and so on. It also means that Red and Green may find it difficult to see eye to eye as do Yellow and Blue. If you look at the descriptions above, you'll see why this might be the case. For example, Yellow is flexible, sociable, and outgoing while Blue is logical, reserved and self-contained. Not the most obvious match, but they can also complement each other.

Beware of broken thumbs

Of course, rules of thumb are made to be broken. Red and Red don't always work so well together. If you think about their style you can see why: the Red style lends itself to being right and in control. When two come together they can't both be right and they can't both be in control at the same time.

The other way rules are broken is due to what we all know – opposites attract. In this instance, people of an opposite style find it helpful, fulfilling and sometimes fun to work and be with others who are very different to them. Reviewing your own diagram, see what applies to you. Who are the people that you naturally connect well with and who are hard work?

Communicate with confidence

These ideas apply to successful teamwork, delighting customers, powerful presentations, effective communication, making projects happen and, of course, how to handle your boss. Just this one chapter is well worth the investment of time you are making by reading this and applying it.

Listening is one of the easiest ways to improve your relationship with others. Look at the situation from their viewpoint. What are their frustrations, interests, fears and ambitions? When you also communicate with them in a way that matches their communication style you are subconsciously creating a much deeper connection with them which will lead to more co-operation. Others will feel that they can get things done with you rather than experiencing disconnection or frustration. Imagine what a difference this makes to your success and enjoyment. You'll be viewed as a skilled communicator who is able to influence decisions and deliver.

> **BIG MENTAL NOTE**
>
> *Gaining the co-operation of others, making decisions and coming to an agreement on a way forward can all be made much easier if you use good questions.*
>
> **| ONE SMALL STEP |**
>
> *Think of one person who you need to work with more successfully. Plan and ask them some questions to understand the world from their viewpoint.*

8 | ATTRACT

Profit from the art of persuasion

If you would win a man to your cause, first convince him that you are his sincere friend.

ABRAHAM LINCOLN

Don't sell let others buy

Have you ever been on the receiving end of someone who talked at you? At a networking event recently, I knew one person only in a room of more than 100 people. I took a look around the room and, spotting a pair of people standing in an open position, I introduced myself into their conversation.

One of the pair wore a special badge, not the one provided by the event. He grudgingly acknowledged me and then said, 'Can I just finish what I was saying?' He was in full flow. He continued with his pitch about a great new business idea, which he aimed mostly at the other person. He talked non-stop, hardly drawing a breath, and then began to direct comments at me as well. His tone was slightly aggressive as was his body language. We listened politely, but as soon as the opportunity came to change the subject, we grabbed it.

If you have a functional role inside an organisation it is easy to think that you are not in sales, but you are. I worked with a group of directors and senior managers responsible for leading big technological change projects. They are a brilliant group of very smart people who keep immense systems running and are at the leading edge of their profession. Of course, most of their stakeholders aren't as forward-looking or comfortable with new technology. What they used to see as a job that was all about inventing solutions and delivering them has become a role that is at least 50 percent persuasion and selling. Without the buy-in they don't even get the chance to show off their bags of tricks.

If the idea of being in sales horrifies you, don't worry. It isn't about hard-nosed sales techniques, but winning hearts and minds. These are the skills you'll learn in this part of the book.

Influencing and persuading others isn't simply a matter of having a strong opinion to share. I suppose a high-pressure sales pitch does work in some settings, but in the knowledge and ideas economy something subtler is more effective. You won't be able to browbeat people into submission. Even if they do say yes on the outside, they'll be saying no on the inside, and when you most need their support you won't get it. Emails, texts and voice messages may be left unanswered.

This is when the 'What's In It For Me?' factor kicks in. Never seek to influence or persuade others to your point of view without first finding out, working out or having a damn good guess at 'What's In It For *Them*?' If you can identify that, instead of having to persuade them they will persuade themselves.

It's been said that it's not that people resist change, but that they resist being changed. You may have embraced lots of change in your life already. When you moved away to university, took your first job or moved in with your first partner, you embraced change. When you started a family you embraced change. All of these have their upside, but there are also lots of downsides that could stop you.

What made you buy in? You sell it to yourself in some way. You think about what the benefits will be for you, your loved ones or your bank balance. You want your experiences to be richer, your relationships to be stronger or your prospects improved. You also don't want to feel like you are losing out or missing an opportunity or getting overlooked. Others operate in a similar way. So don't sell, help them find their reasons for buying.

What did the Greeks ever do for us?

Working in this way involves a few key skills you can easily learn. Aristotle defined persuasion as 'The art of getting people to do something they wouldn't ordinarily do if you didn't ask'. He said influencing others involved three distinct elements.

- Logos
- Ethos
- Pathos

Logos involves the logic of your argument. It involves the presentation of facts and information presented in a methodical way.

Ethos is to do with your credibility and character as the persuader. What people hear when you speak will be influenced to a large degree by your track record.

Pathos refers to the emotion that is roused in the listener. People can be excited, inspired, anxious, motivated, reassured – the list can go on and on – by the way that you speak.

What do you think the result was when I asked a group of senior managers which of these elements they mostly used when seeking to persuade and influence others?

100 percent used logical arguments.

Approximately 60 percent realised the importance of their character and track record.

Only 10 percent gave any thought to how they could enthuse, inspire or excite the group.

Successful persuasion involves all three.

1. Building a logical argument
2. Ensuring that you have ways of demonstrating a track record through experience and or knowledge
3. Connecting with the emotions of the other person or people you are working with.

It seems Aristotle was onto something. Contemporary research by neuroscientists has identified a part of the brain known as the limbic brain. The neocortex is the logical part of the brain which deals with rational, conscious thought and language. The limbic brain processes feelings, motivation, trust and decision-making. When you need to influence and persuade or sell, you can't address the logical and rational alone. You will find that people first 'buy' with their feelings and then they check their decision with their rational mind.

Break the language barrier

On one of my first holidays to Spain in the days when people still sent postcards back to friends at home (quaint I know), I studied the phrasebook and then went into a shop and asked for a stamp. The woman behind the counter looked at me quizzically. Clearly she had not understood what I'd asked for. Then it dawned on her what I meant: I wanted a stamp (a small gummed piece of paper to pay postage), not a stamp (the act of banging down your foot onto something from a raised position). How we laughed!

The thing is, even when you think you are speaking the same language you may not be speaking the same language. This is where you can have problems trying to get things done with others.

Imagine visiting a car dealership to view some cars. The salesperson comes over to you and asks you what you are looking for? You say, 'I want something that looks really sleek and sporty, I want the interior to look smart and sophisticated and my favourite colour is red.'

The salesman takes you over to the latest off-road model. He tells you about the powerful engine and how great it sounds. He even starts it up so that you can hear how impressive it is. Then he invites you to sit inside and listen as he cranks up the powerful sound system. Then he describes how well the noise cancelling works so that you can drive along in almost complete silence on any surface. What's wrong with this?

Research has shown that you have a preference for how you communicate and learn which reflects three of your primary senses: seeing, hearing and touch. These preferences are known as visual, auditory and kinaesthetic. The example above shows a visual request being answered with an auditory explanation, and you can see what a barrier to communication it creates. You could think of another example using touch or movement. Kinaesthetic communicators tend to use phrases, like 'get a grip', 'this doesn't feel right' and 'it's a pain'; auditory communicators will tell you they 'hear what you say' or something is 'clear as a bell'; while visual people will 'see what you mean' or think things 'are looking good'.

Bodywork

Have you ever sat in a restaurant and noticed the people who seem to be getting along with each other and those that don't. Maybe you are sitting in a café or on a train reading this. Watch people who are together and think about how well they seem to be getting on. When people are getting along their body position tends to naturally mirror the other person. They may not even be saying anything, but you can just tell. Subconsciously our bodies synchronise with people we are comfortable with.

Now you know that you can use it to help improve your connection with others and their sense of comfort with you, you can use body language to help your influencing of other people. If, for example, you go into a meeting with someone and they are sitting with their legs crossed and arms folded – do the same. This will create a sense of compatibility between you, even though to begin with it looks hostile or defensive.

If the other person changes to a slightly more relaxed position (perhaps one arm is no longer in the folded position), you can mirror this without exactly copying. If the other person doesn't do this, you can try doing it first and noticing whether they follow your lead. Combined with awareness of their language style, you'll have some advantages when it comes to influencing them. Just as people have a tendency to hire people who are like themselves, they also tend to 'buy' from people they think are like them. Responding to these signals increases their sense of comfort with you.

Persuasion made possible

In 1984, Robert Cialdini, Regents' Professor Emeritus of Psychology and Marketing at Arizona State University, published a book called *Influence: The Psychology of Persuasion*. Everything in the book was researched and tested, and he arrived at six principles. They are worth knowing and applying in your own way. All six of these responses are what he calls 'click, whirr' reactions. Think Pavlov's dog. There is almost a degree of automation to it.

1. Reciprocity
You feel uncomfortable when you feel you owe something to someone and therefore want to repay or reciprocate in some way. Cialdini discovered that even small favours you give to others could trigger this response. What small things could you be doing for people you want to influence positively? Coffee, anyone?

2. Consistency
Cialdini says that you have a desire to act in a way that is consistent. When you have committed to something, you are much more likely to go through with it. Getting commitment from people is much easier if you see it as a series of small yeses. If you get them to make small commitments, especially if it is in a public way, you will get what you want.

3. Social Proof
Simply stated, it means that you like to follow the herd. When you are making decisions you feel more secure when you can see that the product has lots of five star reviews. Someone authoritative may have endorsed it. This principle has come of age even more in the internet age, where services and products live or die by the reviews. How could you make someone feel more secure about a choice or decision by demonstrating that everybody is doing it?

4. Liking
As above, people are more likely to buy from people they see as like themselves, from friends, and from people they know and respect. Cialdini discovered that we're more likely to be influenced by people we like. You can develop this likability in all sorts of ways, even by

giving others compliments. You could just be pleasant and likeable and, together with the strategies you are learning in this book, you'll find that through this you gain their co-operation.

5. Authority

You feel a sense of obligation to people in positions of authority. Doctors in white coats are particularly effective, but other symbols of authority can be as well. How can you underline your authority and expertise? What's your reputation?

6. Scarcity

You want what they can't have. Essentially, things are more attractive when they are limited. You fear losing out on something and so you want it even more. It's the old limited time or limited number offer trick. If people think you are available at the drop of a hat, they won't value your time. If they think your product or service is easy to get and always available they won't be rushing to sign on the dotted line. Increase the scarcity rating of who you are and what you do.

Tune in to *their* needs

Knowing what is important to others makes it far easier to come to win-win agreements. Relationships, projects and 'deals' end up on the rocks because you don't think enough about moulding your proposal or solution to the needs of your colleague or customer.

Tony Robbins speaks about six primary human needs and, whatever you are proposing, you must take these into account. The table below shows the result of meeting the need and what results if you don't. You can see why you don't get support if the needs remain unmet.

Need	Met	Unmet
1. Certainty	Security	No confidence
2. Uncertainty	Variety	Boredom
3. Significance	Status	Unimportant
4. Connection	Involvement	Isolation
5. Growth	Development	No opportunity
6. Contribution	Inspiration	No vision

Imagine the response you will get if you leave people with their needs 'unmet'. The chances of you getting a positive response to your project are very low. Contrast that with how people will act when you meet their needs. The first four are the biggest drivers. Ask yourself what 'security', 'variety', 'status' and 'involvement' mean for that person and the people they represent, in the context of your project, proposal or recommendation.

The art of persuasion isn't new. It's older than Aristotle, but few people bother to learn even the basics. By applying this you will add superior interpersonal skills to your professional talents and it will bring you continued success where others struggle.

BIG MENTAL NOTE

Without buy-in you don't even get the chance to show your expertise.

| ONE SMALL STEP |

Think about how you make people feel. Are you meeting their needs?

9 | GIVE

Give and you'll succeed

Life is most enjoyed when we give ourselves away
ERWIN MCMANUS

Get the habit of helping

You can do everything right that I have described so far, but the world remains an uncertain place. As I began writing this chapter, I received a call from a client who has just been made redundant. He is a dedicated, intelligent and hardworking man who has delivered excellent results and big bottom line benefits for the business. He has worked tirelessly, travelled extensively and given up many weekends. He's the only leader I have ever heard described as honourable. The company was taken over in the last few months by an overseas competitor and part of the cost-saving involves reducing senior headcount.

It's not an unusual tale. He's given it his all, but the situation has changed. There's always a risk when you devote yourself to a role, a team or an enterprise. There aren't any guarantees. Within hours of the news becoming public, he received many messages of goodwill and a number of offers of work. He called to chat about his plans for the next few weeks. My client is known amongst his wide circle as a helper, a listener and a true professional, so the help came flooding in, offering opportunities and displacing the fear that automatically looms at a time like this.

But he wasn't the only one…

Yesterday I received an email from someone I have been reaching out to for the last year, but I've never received a single reply until now. That's okay – if it didn't seem relevant to be in touch I don't mind. I can't remember what my last message said, but this time I got a response. Why? Did I make him an offer he couldn't refuse? No. It seems the reason he replied is he's out of work. He apologised for not having responded to any of my earlier contacts, but now he was open to talk. He only responded when he needed something from me.

Only responding to others when you have a need is the behaviour of dinosaurs of 21st century work. It's a selfish, outdated view of the world. You can't suddenly become active on social networks because you are about to lose your job. Even if you only do one thing every week, reach out beyond your immediate circle. Give someone a tip, a contact or some encouragement. That's just 50 small acts of giving per year.

Don't go it alone

Building those relationships will see you through and your mission starts now. It starts with helping others on their mission, big or small. Helping means using all the skills you have at your disposal, including many of those in this section. Helping doesn't mean running yourself into the ground and losing your own focus. But it will mean taking some time to encourage, assist, politely turn down and do a few favours even when there isn't apparently that much in it for you.

The galaxy of rich relationships you nurture, build and enjoy every day is one of the best ways to put yourself in a position to always have choices and options so you can design your own career. If you have the eyes to see it, there has never been a time quite like this. You have so many opportunities to be free, to work how you want to work doing what you want to do. Retirement is almost dead and, if you love what you do, why would you want to give it up? You can develop your interests, specialisms and working hours to fit the life you want to lead and secure your income – but you won't be able to do it all by yourself.

Value and respect others

Someone once said, 'Be nice to people on the way up because you might need him or her on the way down.' It's not bad advice, even if it is at the cynical end of the scale. The danger is that when your career is going smoothly and you seem to be advancing, you get the idea that it will continue. You may even believe that your talent and hard work will protect you. You easily make the assumption that it is always going to be this way and that you are invulnerable. My client knew that this could change at any time, so he'd done some deep thinking about the next steps he wanted to take and what he wanted from life.

It's never always going to stay the same. It will never just be plain sailing. That's why you need to pay close attention to the network of colleagues, friends, contacts and mentors you are building. It's too easy to forget the person who helped with your C.V., gave you a bit more responsibility, offered you a job or encouraged you along the way.

Whatever you do, don't tread all over others to get what you want. The problem with winning the rat race is that you are still a rat. Your choice, but in this interconnected world it's not the sort of reputation that you want to broadcast. How much effort does it really take to respect your boss for what she is good at? I'll tell you how much. Just about the same as it takes to complain about her. How much effort does it take to forward a useful link or article? What about a text to encourage someone or answer a query?

Crowd source

Why do you think the old boys' network exists? People from certain, schools, clubs and companies learn early on that the easiest way to get on is to be connected to the right people. I'm not advocating nepotism, favouritism or elitism, but there are some lessons to take on board. People in the right networks find each other jobs, they help each other's children and introduce them to others. They help each other achieve much more, more easily than those who try to do it on their own.

I believe in people being rewarded for their achievements and their track record, not simply because of who they know, but more than ever your achievements must include the network you are building online and offline. There are a million ways to connect with others who have similar values, dreams and ideas or know someone who does. Global networks can be built from home and business links forged from your back garden or while you are on the train. You can develop relationships on the phone, through texts, email and Skype. Recent research has shown that it is the weaker links you make which often become the source of help and opportunity. You can make it work for you.

Success is a team game

One of the main settings where you'll be able to build relationships and help others is through the teams you work in. Depending on the style of organisation you are in, this is going to differ. Many teams never even meet each other face to face. They are dispersed across countries and around the world. Many teams are project-based. Some are short term and others longer term. Many involve colleagues from other organisations. This provides you with rich opportunities.

What sort of team player are you?

One of the most misunderstood things about teams is that you must all get on wonderfully. Don't misunderstand me, if it's the opposite of this where people are mistrustful of each other and actively antagonistic it isn't going to work. There has to be trust and co-operation and mutual support. When you ask people about successful teamwork, the pride comes from what has been achieved primarily. They speak about clarity of objectives, leaders who get everyone pulling together, how everyone played their part and used their skills.

Being a team player means committing to shared objectives, finding your specific role in accomplishing them and then reliably doing what you say you will do and helping others to do the same. It's not rocket science.

The wisdom of geese

No matter how much you might try to do it alone, sooner or later you realise you can't achieve true success without the help and support of others. Too much time in isolation or in the wrong place and loneliness sets in, negativity follows and you can find yourself in a downward spiral with ever decreasing opportunities. This can happen even when you are surrounded by a lot of people. Connecting and working with the right people for you lightens the load. A memorable illustration of this is the way flocks of geese behave when they are migrating.

You can draw ideas from many places that instruct and inspire. This analogy is useful when you think about the benefits of relationships and how you and others behave in teams. Here are five facts:

1. As each bird flaps its wings it creates uplift for the birds following it. By flying in a V-formation the flying range for the whole flock is 70 percent greater than if the bird flew alone.
2. Whenever a goose falls out of formation, it suddenly feels the drag and resistance of trying to fly alone and quickly gets back into formation to take advantage of the lifting power of the other birds.
3. When the lead goose gets tired it rotates back into the formation and another goose flies at the point position.
4. The geese honk from behind to encourage those in the front.
5. When a goose gets sick, two geese drop out of formation and follow it down to help protect it.

I worked on these ideas with a newly formed team recently and these are some of the ideas they had for applying it:

- Common agreed vision and way of doing things
- Everyone has a distinct and important contribution
- Be clear about what holds us together
- Take leadership for your thing and volunteer to lead other projects
- Be a problem-solver
- Value the importance of working in the team
- Encourage others verbally and remember to say thank you
- Don't get isolated – keep in touch
- Reach out if someone is struggling

In a follow-up workshop they were able to give examples of how different people had taken the initiative on pieces of work that would normally have been left to the team leader by default. Others were being particularly supportive with a colleague who was struggling to get to grips with a fluid and complicated portfolio.

Opportunities to be a giver appear in some of the more unlikely places and can be the key to becoming very good at something which normally fills you with dread.

*Not*working

No, it's not a typo! In some jobs you may be encouraged to network. The basic idea behind this is that if you network you will be able to tell people what you do and therefore sell. At least that's what you may hear, even if it's not said exactly that way. There's a danger that your interactions with people are coloured by this. This puts you off networking altogether because you don't like the idea of selling and you don't think you're any good at it. Networking's *not* working for you.

It doesn't have to be this way. Use these three simple networking secrets in any situation and you'll build many successful relationships and contacts resulting in unexpected leads, helpful information and, yes, business.

✓ **Prepare**
- Think about simple opening questions to start conversations. 'Have you been to this event before?' No need to launch straight in with 'What do you do?' Find out a little bit about them.
- Find out beforehand who'll be there and who it could be most useful to get to know. Social media makes putting faces to names so much easier and smartphones mean you can do it on the spot.
- Think about how you'll describe what you do in terms of how it benefits others. Instead of 'I'm an accountant', say something useful like 'I save people tax and stress by dealing with the Revenue and the paperwork for them'. Don't get under pressure about the 90-second elevator pitch. Has this ever

happened to anyone in a lift? You're having a conversation, for goodness sake.

✓ **Relax**
- Be human, be yourself and speak to everyone as if they are your friends.
- Approach 'open pairs' and join the conversation by saying 'Hi! Can I join in – I don't know many people here.'
- Remember, it's not about you. Ask questions. Connect first on a normal human level.
- Keep moving by simply saying, 'Great to meet you, I'll let you circulate some more.'

✓ **Nurture**
- *Cards:* Business cards and smartphones are the simplest way to make sure you have the details of people you may want to keep connected to. You don't need to keep them talking all night.
- *Connecting:* Find them on networking platforms and connect. Send them something useful for them and their business.
- *Coffee:* It may be after a few events and exchanges, but some of your contacts will then know enough about you to be willing to meet to chat. Easy as that.

Give and Take

Adam Grant's recent book *Give and Take* reveals some surprising conclusions. He writes that most people operate as *Takers*, *Matchers* or *Givers* and this can be a predictor of how successful you will be – whether you will rise to the top or sink to the bottom. At first sight it looks as though givers lose out, because in a study of a number of different sectors they appear to be the least successful.

But here is the surprise: givers are also the most successful! You may think of givers as those who get taken advantage of, but there is a much more proactive definition. Givers contribute as much as they can without expecting anything in the return. They help others by connecting people and offering mentoring and advice. It is these people who rise above the rest, but, as you will see, you won't be a pushover either.

BIG MENTAL NOTE

The galaxy of rich relationships you nurture, build and enjoy every day is one of the best ways to put yourself in a position to always have choices and options.

| ONE SMALL STEP |

Who can you help or be more generous towards this week?

10 | PUSH

Stand up for yourself

The unreasonable man persists in trying to adapt the world to himself

GEORGE BERNARD SHAW

Welcome to the machine

The world is split into two different types of people. Those that ask for things, and the ones that give them what they want, when they ask. Are those that ask bad people? Well some of them may be, but mostly the problem is with you. In the same way they expect you to say yes, you accept that you are going to say yes. Where does this leave your goals and the things you have to do? What happened to what you want to accomplish?

They ask: you say yes. Simple as that. They ask: you say yes. They ask: you say yes. It's like a drinks machine. They put in the money: out pops the drink. It's mechanical, reliable, dependable, useable. Hold on there. You're not a machine.

'No' can do

Have you ever found it hard to say 'No'?

Especially if it is to your customer, your boss, your colleague, your partner or child… or your friends… or your parents, or your child's friends' parents. Trouble is, the list is getting longer and longer. Your dog? The requests come from so many different directions now. Email, voice message, text, tweets, phone calls, social networks. They add up. They multiply. Could you just do this, that and usually the other as well?

Often it is really hard to say 'No'. I thought I was pretty focused, but then I noticed how often I just agreed to do something for certain people, even though it wasn't part of my schedule or plan. You don't want to be so rigid you can never help someone out, but too often you might be in the habit of just agreeing. There's a big difference between being a giver and being a doormat.

Could you be unintentionally supporting behaviour that you find difficult to deal with? You can train people that it is okay to ask you to do something at a moment's notice because you usually say 'Yes'. You teach people that it is okay to interrupt you because you let them. Perhaps you signal you will drop everything and respond when they've run out of time to do something. I know it's nice to be wanted and needed by others. It makes you feel good. And it makes you feel bad to say 'No'. It's difficult and uncomfortable. If you tend to agree to requests easily and unthinkingly, you find yourself being pulled this way and that. When did you last say 'No' to someone?

Your own plans take second place. Why is someone else's plan or need so much greater than yours? Most people I've worked with who have trouble delivering on time or getting their work done in their working day have a problem with this. You don't know when or how to say 'No.' The pleasure you feel in fulfilling these requests can in time be overcome by the resentment you feel at continually being asked. But it's not their fault; it's not others' behaviour that needs to change, it's yours.

10 steps for No-gotiating

Here are some techniques to help you say 'No'. Most of the time it isn't going to be a straight 'No'. Here are some phrases to help you stand up for yourself. You'll work out which to use when and whether, with the boss or customer, your partner or child.

1. Clarify: When are you hoping to get that by?
2. Quantify: What exactly do you need me to do?
3. Push back: How does that rank compared to the other priority work you've given me?
4. Initiate: I can let you have that by… (under promise – over deliver)

5. Negotiate: I could do this, but not that
6. Give an option: I have some projects I must complete. I could give you 'this' by ____ and 'the final part' by ____
7. Cushion the response: I'd really like to help you with that, but I can't at the moment.
8. Defer: Let me think about it and I'll come back to you on... (Make sure you do)
9. Be reasonable: No, I'm sorry I can't because... (Giving people a reason 'because' is a strong persuader)
10. Say it like it is: No

This can be so unfamiliar and uncomfortable that you might need to experiment just to get used to hearing yourself say these things. Practise in the mirror and record them on your phone and then listen back to yourself. It will soon seem completely natural.

Give your boss a break

One of the hardest people to handle can be your boss. If you have the perfect boss or you are the perfect boss, please contact me on the number at the back of this book. I'd love to know the secret. I have read quite a few psychometric tests of leaders and, do you know what? No one ever got top marks. No one ever returned a faultless assessment. 'Thank you for completing the profiles, but you are perfect! Nothing could possibly improve on who you are now. Everyone, but everyone, thinks you're wonderful.'

The perfect boss just doesn't exist. Just like the perfect employee. Why would you even expect it?

Most things you read on managing upward will have some clever tactics about how to fall into line with your manager's goals and pet projects. They'll teach you how to anticipate their needs and questions and it's all good stuff. No problem there. The sections below make your boss irrelevant for most things you may turn to him or her for now. Most of what your boss does for you, you should be doing for yourself. Follow these simple steps and most of your problems will go away.

STEP 1: MANAGE YOURSELF
The first step in managing your boss is managing yourself. A manager said to me recently that he spends most of his time dealing with the moaning and complaining from his team about recent changes in their company. While we talked, he declined to take a call from a salesman in his team for this very reason. He and the salesperson are caught in a problem that afflicts businesses the world over.

Is it a hangover from school or your parents or something you watched on TV? Where did you get the idea that when you go to work you need someone to instruct you about how to do your work? What happened to behaving as an adult who is responsible, trustworthy and productive? What is going on in your brain, I wonder, that makes you unconsciously dependent on this person called your manager? What are *they* thinking that makes them need to direct what you are doing and know where you are? What an incredible waste of everyone's time and energy.

You have the controls, not your boss.

STEP 2: TREAT YOUR BOSS LIKE YOUR BEST CUSTOMER
If you don't have customers, think about how you like to be treated when you are the customer. Here are six guidelines for treating your boss like your customer. It's all about changing your mindset and then acting in accordance with it.

Mindset 1: Become an expert in their major motivators. What are their frustrations, interests, fears and ambitions?
Mindset 2: Always think at least one step ahead.
Mindset 3: Your ambition should be to never have your boss chase you.
Mindset 4: Solve problems rather than ask for solutions.
Mindset 5: Know what makes them happy.
Mindset 6: No-gotiate.

The age of 'unmanagement'

I sometimes hear complaints about micromanagement. If you are a leader and you are micromanaging your people, please stop it now. If you are checking their whereabouts, the hours they are spending where and doing what, and constantly reviewing what they achieved and how they are doing their job, you are both in serious need of help.

Unless you are running a cotton-mill in the north of England in the late 1800s, and I suspect you are not, it is a destructive and self-defeating practice. You either have the wrong person in the job and therefore you need to find a way to help them find a more suitable role inside or outside your organisation, *or* you both have a very poor idea of how this relationship is supposed to work. See if you can make it work better.

Four principles of productive 'unmanagement':

1. The individual is in the role because they have shown some reasonable degree of skill, aptitude and attitude which makes them suitable.
2. This being the case, it is your job to help them clearly understand the expectations and results of the role and encourage, challenge, support them so that they can do their very best and fulfil their potential.
3. The rest is down to them. They may not 'get it' at first, but it is your job to help them 'get it' and once they've 'got it' you can have a productive professional relationship.
4. Iron out the bumps and challenges along the way together.

Propose solutions don't present problems

In what was a memorable meeting for me, and a turning point for my client, I could not believe my ears at first. This relatively senior person, let's call him Dave, should have been giving his boss, Mary, a progress report on current critical projects and the development of the team.

What followed was a bleeding heart tale of problems, difficulties, conundrums and pleas for help. Yes, I am being a bit harsh, although it's not far off the truth. Dave is well paid and operates at a senior level. It was important to get to the bottom of this behaviour. There was an unhealthy dependence and neediness in Dave. He thought it was okay to come to that meeting with problems, expecting Mary to take his troubles on board to relieve him of the thinking and resolve that was required to create solutions and actions.

I had the opportunity to coach Dave after this meeting and, when I told him what I'd observed, it resulted in a whole change of approach affecting him deeply and lastingly. Dave just nailed a more senior role. Go Dave!

I'm sure that you've never been that extreme, but notice how it can creep into your approach. Managers don't have all the answers. They may have some knowledge they need to convey to you. They may have some experience which is important, but they are just one of the sources of information you need to interrogate. They may have guidance for you that you don't have access to, but they are not the font of all knowledge, they are not your counsellors, and they are not your parents or your teacher. Stop treating them as if they are.

Here's how it works

It is not your manager's job to make sure you are doing your work. It's yours. It's not your manager's job to tell you how to sort out problems. It's not your manager's job to give you little pats on the back and check that you are okay. Good managers do this kind of thing, but you are responsible for your own work, deadlines, skills, state of mind, health and relationships.

Let's use the performance/personal development review as an example. Do you go into these meetings having given little or no serious thought to your own achievements, areas for improvement or ideas for projects and opportunities that could stretch you? Have you got into the habit of expecting your manager to take the lead in these meetings? Next time, surprise them. Be prepared: review yourself in advance and go to the meeting raring to go.

--- BIG MENTAL NOTE ---

Why is someone else's plan or need so much greater than yours? Most people who have trouble getting their work done in their working day have a problem with this.

| ONE SMALL STEP |

Look back at the Mindset list and choose one or two to implement. Number 4 is a good one.

# 11 | SWERVE

Stop working the hard way

What we see depends mostly on what we look for
JOHN LUBBOCK

Easy riders?

Did you ever cycle with someone sitting on the saddle while you were doing all the peddling and the steering? Even if you've only watched, you'll know that it is slow, wobbly and inefficient. It looks like an accident waiting to happen. The peddler on the front soon gets exhausted. The one on the back has a mixed expression somewhere between smugness and fear. It doesn't really do either any good and they could probably walk faster.

When you see this, your sympathy usually goes to the person doing the peddling. Well you are either sympathetic or you think, 'What an idiot'. Why are they doing all that hard work and letting the person on the back have an easy ride? You reserve your admiration for the person on the back. How did they talk that person into doing all the hard work?

It's hard doing the work of two people, or three or four. You can't keep going like that for long. I come across this all the time. You might think that it is less senior people who have the biggest problem with this. Strangely, it is often the team leaders, managers and senior people who fall into this trap. No wonder you are stressed.

Liberate yourself

If you are a manager or team leader, did you feel like your job doubled when you took on that role? You still had your own work, but then you had all this other stuff. Some of that other stuff is to do with policies and regulations and all the things that have to be done legally when you employ people. Then there are the other things that seem to involve wiping noses and putting plasters on knees and answering questions and having an open door policy. They might involve people falling out with each other or not co-operating or being unaccountable.

Now is the time to take stock of your approach. Remember, in a previous chapter you read about how you train others how to treat you. Well this could be you. Your whole leadership style could change as a result of this chapter. You could save hours and hours of your own time by starting to treat your team as responsible and capable people who have the capacity to resolve 80 percent or more of their own issues. Many people are conditioned to this contrary relationship with a manager or team leader and, if they can get you to do the work for them, they will.

Now you are in serious danger of not having enough to do. Ha, ha, ha! I hear you laugh. What would you do if you could free up more of your time because you no longer mop up after everyone else? Now you can really think about where you add value as a leader and manager. Make sure you are delivering value in your own right.

Stop doing their job

I was coaching Mark, a technical director in a consultancy, and one of his main struggles was with time management. At least he thought that was the problem. Mark was clearly quite stressed. He was juggling a young family, a building project at home and the daily challenges of his technical role with the new responsibilities as a senior leader in the company. When he started to describe what was happening and everything that was eating up his time, it soon became apparent that he didn't have a problem with time management, he had a problem with doing others' work for them.

The nature of their work involved writing technical reports. Site surveys, investigations, studies and data are all compiled to provide expert analysis and advice. The report has to be accurate because it informs important and costly decisions about building and infrastructure projects. It is important to get it right.

Frequently, less qualified employees write less complex reports that are checked and approved by the senior consultant. Tony does this type of work in Mark's team. The problem for Mark is that Tony consistently produces substandard reports that have basic errors in them such as spelling and grammar mistakes as well as technical shortcomings that he should have spotted himself.

What did Mark do? Like many good managers he corrected the mistakes in Tony's report. This continued through a number of iterations of Mark correcting and Tony making the changes until, after three or four attempts, the report was ready to send to the client, but not without some final polishing from Mark.

And so it goes on...

Disastrous! Think about the consequences.

- Mark is doing Tony's work for him
- Clients are unhappy because deadlines are missed
- Mark's time is wasted on work below his expertise level
- Fewer hours charged at Mark's high rate
- Tony is being trained to be lazy and dependent
- The working relationship between Mark and Tony is strained
- Mark's boss is dissatisfied with the performance of his team
- Mark's wife is unhappy about the long hours and the work he is bringing home
- Tony isn't learning, improving or growing

Misguided management

If you asked 100 managers and leaders what management is all about, a good proportion of the answers would talk about giving advice, imparting knowledge and supporting staff. The way this plays out is that, more often than not, when a member of staff has a question or a problem, you believe you are supposed to come up with the answer. So do they; that's the job, isn't it? This is what our manager did for us. Managers know more: they have the experience, they can tell us what to do.

I agree this all sounds good, and in some circumstances it is what you should do. It should be the exception rather than the rule. If you asked those same managers how they learned to do things, they'd probably answer – through having to do it themselves or by learning from mistakes. If your default view of management is about having all the answers, it is time to stop, re-evaluate and try a different style that will be more liberating.

Lost opportunities

The problem is that this style of management is hard on you and unhelpful for the other person. In the short term it can seem easier just to spout the answers. At the time you feel good about being the font of all knowledge. But no one is growing. You are building reliance and stifling initiative. It starts to become noticeable when you expect projects to be started or pushed on, but they are not. You are probably filling your inbox too. Instead of people being self-starters, they seem to need someone to kick-start them.

I was once helping my son with his homework. The homework involved him building a model of a volcano. So we got to work with the papier-mâché and paint and created a fine looking volcano. At the end when I asked him if he was pleased he looked up at me sadly and said, 'It feels like you did it all for me'. There are a lot of messages in that little phrase and I have not forgotten them. Ouch!

It could have been a great opportunity for him to be proud of his own work and to learn more skills, but I got in the way. I did it for him.

Wrong way to pick up the pieces

You'll encounter this whether you are a manager or not. Frequently people produce work that's below par, not exactly what is needed, incomplete or in some other way lacking. So what do you usually do? The answer isn't what you might expect. Incredibly, more often than not you decide to do it yourself. As if you didn't have enough to do. And do you know what – they know this is what you are going to do.

I have worked with very senior people who are sent documents with everything from spelling mistakes to poor structure and logic, and they correct it all, often working late and eating up family and important downtime. Some colleagues assume they will do this and others are astounded that they have.

It is so easy to feel that you ought to take up the slack, pick up the pieces and sort things out for others. Don't! Especially when you are one of the super-conscientious, high achieving, hard working types. You may even start making excuses for them. Surprisingly, you quickly start questioning your own performance. Did you tell them the deadline? Did you make your expectations clear?

It won't work upside down

Like most pens, you don't work very well if you are trying to do it upside down. Can you see how this is all based on a system that requires you to make sure the other person is doing their job properly and that you are doing everything you can to compensate for that? This isn't good for you or them; this is when things get all upside down and you start doing others' work for them.

Result? You get more under pressure, probably a bit resentful and they go down a little in your estimation because they didn't come up to scratch again. Your 'To do list' grows longer and the team member or colleague doesn't change or grow or improve. You have probably never understood what was going on. You think it is what you are supposed to do as a manager. Help people do their jobs, but that so easily turns into doing it for them.

Wouldn't it be liberating if it didn't have to be this way? What if you could stop picking up the pieces and work in a way with others that meant they took responsibility for their own work in all its aspects; if you could learn the skills to ensure that you did your work and they did theirs in a way that met expectations and delivered the results.

No pain, no gain

Lots of the strategies in this book could help with this problem, whether you are a manager or not. What I can promise is that there will be a learning curve for you and others when you start responding differently.

You will worry about hitting the deadlines and the quality of the work produced. They may feel a bit under pressure to begin with. You might even feel a bit insecure because you've got used to this role of supervisor cum teacher who corrects others' work. Resolve to go through the pain barrier and do more of the work that you are uniquely able to do. If taking this approach frees you up – that's the point. If it leaves a bit of a vacuum – that's excellent. You need to be free to do the things that excite you and where you add real value. It's time to raise the bar.

With the application of key skills, a little guidance and perseverance you will begin to see fantastic results. Hand in hand with this, take a new look at delegation.

The modern art of delegation

It *is* a modern art because you are probably working in a much flatter, less hierarchical organisation than 10 or even five years ago. Delegation used to be about assigning tasks to subordinates for them to complete. Achieving projects is now about successful collaboration and teamwork with diverse, interrelated parts fulfilling their role. It isn't a case of telling people what to do, but skilfully engaging them so that they own achieving results with enthusiasm.

Whether between colleagues or with someone who reports to you, use this simple R3 approach to make sure you aren't left to pick up the pieces. Use the coaching approach discussed in Chapter 13 rather than a 'tell' approach

✓ **R1 Result**
- Describe the context, or ask them to, and then agree what is the result that needs to be achieved.
- Discuss expectations about what a good result looks like, including deadlines.
- Agree where the lines are drawn in terms of their authority to decide and when they need to ask you.

- Most of it should come from them with you commenting and asking questions so that you have confidence you are going to receive what you want.
- The amount of time and detail will depend on the ability and experience of the person in the project.

✓ R2 Review

Agree when you will review progress and how (written or verbal). It must be clear that the responsibility to put this in the diary, run the meeting etc. is theirs not yours. The review should include progress report, any difficulties encountered and their plans for resolving any hiccups, next steps etc.

✓ R3 Resources

Check what they are going to need to get this done. What do they need help with? What will you do? How can you help them get their own help? Focus also on the personal and professional developmental aspects of them doing this.

See others in a different way

In the 1960s, Douglas McGregor put forward his theory of motivation and management which involved Theory X and Theory Y styles of management. Theory X managers see people as workshy, lazy and irresponsible. Theory Y managers see people as hardworking, responsible and problem solvers. People will tend to respond in accordance with the way that you see and treat them. If you view them as incapable, you will treat them that way and they will act accordingly. If you view them as people with the potential to take responsibility and do well, they will respond to this positively. Many studies have backed up this general approach. It's a no-brainer: it brings out the best in others and allows you to be excellent at what you do.

> **BIG MENTAL NOTE**
>
> *You could save hours and hours of your own time by starting to treat your team as responsible and capable people.*
>
> **| ONE SMALL STEP |**
>
> *Use the R3 delegation process.*
> *(It doesn't have to be with a team member – adapt it for peers and even your boss)*

12 | SPARKLE

Do it with style

It's never too late to become the person you might have been
GEORGE ELIOT

Zero gravitas

It is said, 'You can't judge a book by its cover'. So why do publishers spend so much time designing great book covers and creating enticing titles? Simply because you *do* judge a book by its cover. Even in this day of the e-book, I find myself squinting at small black and white illustrations on a first generation Kindle. These tiny graphics send messages to my brain and, along with a cluster of other triggers, still have an effect on my purchasing decisions. People buy books because of their title, because what is on the outside sends messages about what's on the inside.

A friend and I were chatting about a mutual acquaintance. It was a very positive discussion. The changes taking place in the organisation where we both worked at the time were extremely challenging and we commented on the work ethic and commitment of our mutual contact. Then he said, 'When I think of Sarah I think of her red face and watching her rush around.'

Sarah was a pretty senior person and ambitious to go higher, so what impression was she creating with this influential colleague? Whether you like it or not, it isn't just the quality of your work, your devotion to the role or even how clever you are that guarantee the impression you make on others. How you package yourself and appear to them has tremendous impact.

My friend saw Sarah as a rusher-around, a worker bee and a doer. The clues are as much in what he did not say about her. He didn't comment on her calmness or her presence and natural authority. This is what is happening to you all the time. People are continually making judgements about you, your suitability for promotion or certain projects or clients from the signals that they have available to them.

They are deciding whether you fit in their team, company or at the top table by using a speedy filtering system based on a number of pre-judgements. You are giving out these signals all the time and, just as your written signature is distinctive, so is the collection of signals you are giving out on a daily basis. This is happening to you now. It is better to be aware and prepared.

Image rights

Although we are going to be talking about how you appear to others on the outside, it starts on the inside.

In Part One you read about uncovering your purpose, defining your values and mapping out your own path. There are no short cuts. By doing these things you'll have an internal driving force which will be the most powerful element contributing to the lasting impression you make on others. The last thing you want is for all that great stuff to be undermined by the way you look or sound or interact.

Marshall McLuhan said, 'The medium is the message'. It isn't just about the content, but the way the content is delivered that has an enormous bearing on how it is received. Because you believe what you are a trying to achieve in the world is important, you spend time ensuring that what appears on the outside is as influential as it can be. Inside and outside should fit together. It's called congruence. It's crucial to give plenty of attention to the things that will determine the experience others have of you and the memory they will take away. Whatever your business, position, ambition or role – this is significant.

If you're going to space walk you'd better be dressed for it

This is all part of your preparation for your mission. It means you have to pay attention to your:

- ✓ Voice
- ✓ Dress/Hair
- ✓ Hygiene
- ✓ Energy
- ✓ Body language
- ✓ Eye contact
- ✓ What you say
- ✓ How you say it
- ✓ Listening
- ✓ Posture
- ✓ Facial expressions
- ✓ Handshake
- ✓ Gestures

To simplify this, think of it in terms of *Voice* and *Body*.

Give yourself a 'Voiceover'

Let's take this one first. What do you think is important about your voice? If you are going to make the best impression on others how will you need to speak?

I coached a manager in her 30s a few years ago, and sometimes you realise that, as a coach, you need to address an area that you suspect others haven't. This woman was bright and articulate and creative. She had some great ideas for improving skills and competencies in her organisation, but she wasn't being heard. The curious thing about her was that she spoke with a surprisingly childish voice. Almost a cartoon character-style voice. Not all the time, but a lot.

One day during one of our meetings I tentatively broached the subject. Now it's one thing to be sensitive, but at some point you have to say what's on your mind. Thankfully, we'd built up enough trust and she was receptive. It transpired that her altered voice had become a habit due to lack of confidence. What appeared on the outside came from what was on the inside. She betrayed her lack of confidence and her diminished view of herself in her voice. As she practised in the security of the coaching meetings, she altered her voice (back to normal) and as a result became more plausible and convincing. Years later I met her again – no more Minnie Mouse. Fantastic!

If, when you speak with people, you tend to be tentative or apologetic the impression you are creating is that of an uncertain person. If you are opinionated, inflexible and non-listening you are creating the impression of a pig-headed and stubborn person. You can see how this works. Sometimes it's okay to be your own worst critic, or ask a trusted friend, colleague or manager to get some feedback.

For you it could be your tone or speed or volume. Speak clearly, vary your pace, volume and tone. Don't mumble. Keep it interesting. Get the basics right. Here's an easy way to remember it – V.A.P.E.R. It's what comes out of your mouth.

Volume
Articulation
Pitch
Emphasis
Rhythm or pace

Say hello to people, give them the time of day and thank them when it is appropriate. Although the rules of good manners are much more relaxed now, be polite, respectful and well-mannered.

It may be your choice of words that's significant. Remember you are communicating for the other person's benefit, so make sure you're not using too much management speak or jargon. Pretty much everywhere I have been, with the odd exception, swearing in a public work context is not acceptable. Then, of course, discriminatory language is absolutely off-limits. Gossiping, moaning and back-stabbing are rarely constructive or helpful to your own cause. If you gossip and moan to one person about another, who is to say you won't gossip about each other. What are your standards? Know them and keep them.

Never forget to ask good questions and listen attentively. Most people feel they've had a great conversation with you if they have talked about themselves and their areas of interest.

Check your 'Bodybrand'

Here are six 'body checks':

1. **Smell nice.** One of my early responsibilities as a manager meant that I had to speak to a person older than me about body odour. Yes, I drew the short straw! A number of colleagues who worked alongside this man mentioned the unpleasant scent that emanated from him. Save everyone else the trouble and pay attention to your personal hygiene without overpowering them with perfume. Make sure you don't have bad breath, that your teeth are clean and your hair is cut, washed and styled.
2. **Dress suitably** for your work place. Keep your shoes clean and smart. I worked with an M.D. who judged the validity of someone who came in to buy out his company by the quality of his shoes. The shoes were shoddy and so was the deal. As a rule, choose one notch smarter rather than one notch more casual.
3. **Connect with confidence.** You will impress people as a confident person if you look them naturally in the eye and shake them firmly by the hand. Be sensitive to the handshake of individuals that may not be as strong as your own, or vice versa, and respond accordingly. It helps to build rapport. Continue to look people in the eye when they are speaking.
4. **Positive posture.** As you read earlier, body language is a key to building relationships with others. If your posture is slumped or slouched, whether sitting or standing, you are giving messages of tiredness, lack of energy and drive. Your posture should normally be upright without looking as though you have a plank of wood strapped to your back.
5. **Express yourself.** If you are enthusiastic about something, let your face know. Of course there are times in business when it's wise not to give away too much, but don't make that your

default. You are a human being not a robot. Your expressiveness can also reach your hands and arms. You probably don't want to look like a frantic mad scientist, but more expansive gestures that express ideas tend to be read as signs of confidence.

6. **Stay fit**. Whatever your ambitions, you'll need energy and a reasonable amount of good health, so look after yourself. It's odd how sometimes the busier you get the less attention you pay to your health, energy and fitness. There are always good excuses, but effective workouts can now be done in just a few minutes a day using plyometric exercises. So no excuse really.

If you've always meant to get rid of those few extra pounds, or maybe more than a few, get to work on it now. Don't delay another week. It will do wonders for your self-esteem. People will shower you with compliments as you slim down. You will be more respected because many people struggle to make this change. But, if you are going to be a high flyer and enjoy it rather than send yourself to an early grave, make a plan to get fit.

Lead without the label

To stand out from the crowd you have to stand out from the crowd. Don't expect to be invited into the circles of power if you haven't stepped up first. Let go of all those outdated views of leadership that you have been carrying around in your head.

Huge amounts of paper, ink and footage are devoted to the idea of the heroic leader. Business writers and the media perpetuate the idea of a special category of person whose innate brilliance sets them apart. They are often visionary, charismatic, bombastic and not to be trifled with. In short they are regarded as born leaders. A poll in 2006 revealed that about half the CEOs of the Fortune 500 companies were white and tall (just under six feet), compared to an average male at five feet, nine inches. Shocking – why are they more capable of leading?

The spectacular failures of some of these acclaimed leaders at Enron, WorldCom, RBS and other financial giants don't always get the coverage they should. Leaders of this type appear almost unassailable until their massive failings are revealed.

There are, and have undoubtedly been, great leaders, but every generation is tempted to automatically revere the success stories of the day. Don't be misled by the idea of great superstar leadership. The aim of this book is for you to bring the best out of yourself and believe that you can achieve anything that you really want if you'll believe in yourself and put in the effort to accomplish it.

Be your own kind of hero

You may think of leadership as a position of privilege that is given to those who are different or better than you, and that leadership is about climbing the greasy poll to someone's idea of what constitutes success. If this is what you want out of leadership, my advice is give up now. Ask anyone who is leading and managing people and they'll tell you it has its joys and sorrows. It's challenging when you put your head above the parapet.

Here's a quick checklist to help you think about whether leadership is for you:

- Are you genuinely interested in creating success for yourself and others?
- Do you want to inspire, envision, encourage and help?
- Do you aim to bring out the best in others and help them bring out the best in themselves?
- Do you want to help people achieve greater things together than they can apart?
- Is leading a privilege to be earned and not a right?
- Do you want to develop and contribute your best qualities for your own fulfilment and success, as well as others?
- Are you focused on vision, direction and results, not only the process?
- Do others tend to follow you?

Clearly this isn't an exhaustive list, but if you can challenge your own motivation it's a great starting place. If you can answer 'Yes' to most of these, it could be that leading people is for you. Whatever else you need in terms of skills and knowledge can almost certainly be learned.

Earn the right

If the very idea of anyone following your lead in anything absolutely terrifies you, there's no need to put yourself under that kind of pressure. There are all sorts of ways to lead, and the opportunities and potential rewards are greater than ever. Leadership is constantly evolving. I once heard an American speaker who was a bit of a jock in his college days talk about how he used to laugh at the guys who walked around with seventeen pens in their shirt pockets, only to realise that now the geeks run the world! Who saw that coming? The geeks, probably.

Organisations are flatter and less hierarchical. There are fewer positions to be promoted to. Recognition and reward comes more from the results you achieve than the position you hold. This is great news for you. You don't have to be an all singing, all dancing heroic leader in order to show leadership in the projects, teams and technical challenges that excite you. You earn the right and recognition by stepping up.

In fact, if you are going to boost your enjoyment and prospects and opportunities, this is exactly what you should be thinking about now. You can either just keep functioning day in, day out, doing what is expected of you, or you can start to think about what motivates and excites you and show some initiative. What is known as 'command and control' is dead in our knowledge and ideas economy. Alongside the people skills you've already read about in this book, you should be thinking about how you are taking your business forward in terms of your new thinking and expertise.

Act as if

There's some benefit from completing checklists. They make you think but, a little bit like eating oysters, you can't really know if you like leadership until you've tried it – and even then sometimes you have to have a little chew on it before you really know.

You have to try it on for size.

You may not feel like a leader. It's often very difficult to feel it until you actually do it. Whatever the next challenge or opportunity seems to be, step into it confidently. Act as if you are before you have any kind of official position, and before you know all the answers. Lead without the label.

Think about a manager or leader you respect. They don't have to be 100 percent solid gold. Just consider some of their better qualities and without appearing to be some strange fanatical replicant, emulate some of the qualities that you respect. Walk the walk and talk the talk.

Stretch yourself

If you are working in any white collar, knowledge-based role or business, and you have any ambition (which I assume is at least one of the reasons you are reading this book), then you have to show leadership. I'm not talking about the next promotion. I mean now.

It's not okay to sit in the team meeting and say nothing. It's not okay to wait for others to ask before you speak, plan, solve, suggest or take some initiative. You need to be leaderly! Not bossy or taking the lead when it isn't yours to take. But when there are opportunities to think and behave as if you were leading, and there are plenty because most people are sitting back waiting to be told, you need to grab them. You'll find yourself flying past others who have simply missed the importance of this.

How are you going to stretch yourself? How are you going to challenge yourself? What interesting, or sometimes not quite so interesting, project is out there that you could get your teeth stuck into? Often, all it needs is a little creative thinking to work out how you can use something to connect with some stimulating people, or as an opportunity to learn or impress. If you are flexible and willing, you'll soon build a favourable reputation.

One of the indicators of your leadership abilities is the balance you strike between doing and getting things done. You may be thinking, 'What another project? I simply can't do any more!' How do you think leaders with large portfolios get things done? How do they keep on top of everything? Well there are myriad reasons, but here's one. When they take something on they are usually thinking, 'How can I get that done?' rather than, 'How am I going to do it?' A big part of your success will depend on your ability to bring out the best in others, and that is what I will help you with next.

BIG MENTAL NOTE

It's crucial to give plenty of attention to the things that will determine the experience others have of you and the memory they will recall when you aren't there.

| ONE SMALL STEP |

Expand your horizons. Find a good opportunity to take the lead in something that isn't part of your usual portfolio.

13 | PEP!

Why it pays to make others look good

We are here to help one another along life's journey
ELEANOR ROOSEVELT

Work smarter

As I move around working in different businesses and organisations, I see more and more being asked of fewer people, often without any more reward. If you are going to continue to be successful in a demanding business environment, you will probably need to find some ways to work smarter not just harder and faster. Nelson D. Rockefeller asked, 'Why do the work of a thousand men when I can put a thousand men to work?' You still lack some of the skills that can make management easier and more pleasurable. If managing and getting things done with others can be made easier, I'm all for it.

One of the key distinctions often drawn in terms of leadership styles is between transactional leadership and transformational leadership. Transactional leadership focuses on people doing what they are paid for. You can see where it got this name. You do what you are meant to do and you get paid for it. It's a transaction.

Transformative leadership is thinking all the time about how things can develop and improve for the future, particularly for the people who are involved. A transformative leader is always asking, 'How can we grow, learn and be better through these experiences?' When you are trying to get things done, put your transformative hat on. But these ideas are not for leaders only. If you want to know how to make things move in all sorts of situations, adopt this approach.

Use the magic of a coaching approach

Coaching is a tremendous tool for helping individuals and teams develop. You don't have to be a highly trained, fully accredited coach to be able to use a coaching methodology for great results. One of the best ways to make your own job easier is to learn to use a coaching method in your interactions with others. The applications are numerous. Please note the distinction I am making here: I am suggesting that you use a coaching approach in your interactions with people; I am not telling you to be everyone's coach. But you can use the wisdom of coaching to make your life easier and you will help others to be more effective and productive as well.

People tend to be more resistant when they are told what to do. The strange thing is this can even be the case when they've asked for help. Have you ever noticed those non-committal 'ers' and 'ums' when someone has asked you for an opinion or an idea and it clearly hasn't quite come up to scratch in their judgement?

The same rule of thumb applies whether you need them to get them to do something because you are in a manager or leadership role of some sort, or if they have come to you for advice. Stop telling people what to do. Telling people what to do encourages lazy thinking on their behalf. You want people to think for themselves, not be dependent on you. You should stretch your qualities as a leader by practising the art of bringing out the best in others.

The basic idea of coaching is that you help other people find solutions for themselves and commit to them. It's about their growth and fulfilling their own potential. It involves dealing with the present and finding options to move forward. What a great idea for you and them. You make your work harder by feeling that you have to persuade other people, but it is much easier to let people persuade, direct and motivate themselves. Many books have been written about coaching, so I am going to give you some of the basics for you to use constructively, without having to claim you are a coach.

If you are going to use this approach, you must have a fundamental belief in the capacity and potential of others to solve their own problems. You are not the font of all wisdom. You'll need to be skilful at structuring a conversation, at asking good questions and listening well.

Ignite their potential with S.P.A.R.K.

STEP 1 S: SUCCESS
Focus on the outcome
It starts with helping someone to clearly identify what he or she is trying to achieve. Of course there is usually a challenge, task or problem in hand that needs to be dealt with in some way. The tendency is to focus first on the problem rather than the result you want. Once you know what the conversation is about instead of asking about the problem ask, 'What would be a good result?' or 'What is it you're trying to achieve?'

Think of the meetings you have been in when the problem or issue at hand is discussed at length, but few decisions are reached. You could save yourself and everyone else a huge amount of time simply by asking, 'What are we really trying to achieve here?' Without taking over in an inappropriate way, you can guide the conversation toward useful actions.

It's much better to help them envision success. If you start to see the prospect of a successful outcome, what happens to your levels of energy and motivation? They go up. When you start feeling motivated and energised, what happens to your levels of creativity? They go up. So help other people to get into this state.

STEP 2 P: PROBLEM
Clarify the challenge or problem
Once the individual or the group is in a solution focused state, you can start to investigate the problem. Remember, the important thing is to focus on the present. No one can solve the past. I realise there is always context that is important, but it is so easy for people to waste your time and theirs, your energy and theirs by regurgitating the past like a vinyl record that has got stuck. I am frequently amazed at how even more senior people who should know better want to go over and over old information and difficulties; 99 percent of the time it is useless.

Have you noticed how much time you can spend discussing problems with people. You go round and round the problem, but the facts of the problem are only relevant in as much as they affect the result you are trying to achieve. So don't waste time discussing aspects of a problem or challenge that aren't relevant. If you spend too much time on the problem, there's a risk it becomes your problem not theirs. This is the exact opposite of what should be occurring.

Ask questions about what is actually happening now. Who is being affected? What is the effect? How many people? When? Be specific. Your goal is to help them focus on the current problems, the facts and the effects. Here are some other questions you could ask them.

- What is the impact of this problem?
- What have you done about this so far?
- Which specific team is not working well? In what way?
- Which process is breaking down? How often? Under what circumstances?

Remember. You are not asking these questions because you are trying to find the answer to the problem. You may be part of a group or team that has to find the answer, but in this case you are helping facilitate the group. If you are speaking with an individual, the idea is that you are working with them so that they discover solutions for themselves.

Clarifying the facts is important because there can be a tendency to speak in generalisations about problems. 'Our marketing isn't working.' 'The website is rubbish.' 'The team meeting is a waste of time.' These are the sorts of things that people will say. It's the sort of thing you say. But you will only resolve the real issue if you identify the real problem. Very often the process of asking for facts helps the other person identify where the problem really lies and the possibilities of a solution begin to emerge. At this point you can begin to encourage them to consider solutions.

STEP 3 A: ALTERNATIVES
Create options
You can easily get stuck at this point because your group, or the individual you are speaking with, will grind to a halt trying to think of

the perfect solution to the problem. Most challenges and problems are not solved in one mighty bound. Neither is there only one perfect solution. There are a number of possible solutions.

Resist the temptation to provide the answer. Don't undo all that good work. The point of using this approach is to save you time by helping other people get into the habit of using their own capabilities and intellect to solve their own problems. Remind them about the result they said they wanted to achieve. Ask them what they could *possibly* do to make some progress toward the result they want. The word *possibly* is vital. It opens up the mind to a number of ideas and options. Don't be afraid of silence. Let them think. They have an amazing computer inside their heads and instincts for the right way to go, and you must encourage them to use them.

This stage is about idea generation. How many possible ways of moving closer to their desired outcome can they think of? When they have come up with some ideas simply ask them, 'What else could you try?' That word 'try' is like *possibly*. It is encouraging them to think creatively and experimentally. You will find that people get stuck because they don't try anything different and because their brains have closed down to thinking of new options.

Even if they don't come up with what you would have done, that's fine. Unless you think they are missing something really important that will definitely land them or others in hot water, keep quiet. They might have to go and make a mistake or two just like you did.

STEP 4 R: REVIEW
Confirm the process
It's useful at this point to briefly review where you have come from and where you have got to in the conversation because the next stage is all about making a commitment. Repeating the outcome or the goal re-energises them before they contemplate their next steps. Restate the specific problem and the ideas they have created to move forward.

It's a good time to check that the conversation is making sense for them and to encourage them. If there are any obstacles that could get in their way, flush them out now. Sometimes someone will go through the whole conversation through to making a commitment without mentioning something that is holding him or her back. Get it out in the open now so you can encourage more ideas that will help them to overcome that issue.

STEP 5 K: KICK-START
Pledge to action
Now it is time to help them commit to what they are actually going to do. Out of all the options they have created, what are they going to do? What is their preferred way forward? Ask them what they are going to do, by when and with whom. Ask them how they will make the decision and the timeframe known to others because, as we've seen, people who make a public commitment are much more likely to follow through. At this point you may want to ask them whether they need any help from you or others to successfully deliver the result.

Use your judgement
You can imagine that there are times when this approach can be frustrating for others. It is not a universal approach to be used with absolutely every problem, conversation or issue. Sometimes people just need a quick piece of information, advice or guidance, but you will begin to notice that there are plenty of conversations where you can help people think for themselves.

This approach does not have to be time consuming, as you begin to become more confident in the way that you use it. Keep the five steps in mind and it will become natural for you to apply this structured approach in your own thinking, in meetings and in conversations with others. It will save you time and energy and get you to results quicker. People will appreciate the way in which you've helped them and others will notice that you often help meetings and discussions come to a positive conclusion. Say goodbye to going around the houses at meetings.

Health warning

It won't all be plain sailing: some people enjoy talking about problems. They like to complicate things and share the extent of their in-depth knowledge about problems. People like this are part of the problem and it is in their interests to make sure that the problem seems terribly complicated and difficult. It's what keeps them in a job. It gives them the opportunity to write long emails and reports which waste your time. They won't like the solution-based approach you are encouraging, so beware. Don't get drawn in to their way of doing things. There's always another way.

Prepare to be appreciated

Using coaching can be one of the most rewarding skills you have. I've had the privilege of coaching people and teaching others how to use it as an approach and the results are often nothing short of remarkable. To see other people become more fulfilled and energised by their role and blossom as individuals is a wonderful thing. You often receive appreciative feedback, but the best feedback is seeing how people change.

You are learning the mindset and skills that will help you to turn your potential and talents into lasting success. Part One was all about building your personal momentum, defining your purpose and clarifying your goals. Part Two gives you the interpersonal skills to excel with people, enabling you to build trust, support and enthusiasm time and again. Part Three equips you with essential skills to keep you at the top of your game. They have been chosen because after 12 years of training and coaching high potential and senior individuals and teams I have seen what it takes for people to keep going and deliver consistent outstanding performance. Within a few concise chapters you can quickly and easily learn how to get and stay ahead.

―――― **BIG MENTAL NOTE** ――――

You should stretch your qualities as a leader by practising the art of bringing out the best in others.

| ONE SMALL STEP |

Instead of telling someone how to do something, use S.P.A.R.K. to encourage them to find a solution for themselves. Tell them what you are working on and why first.

STOP - GROW - FLOW Chart (2)

PART TWO

Chapters 7-13

Review each chapter and make a quick note of a thought or page number under each heading. Don't write too much. The trick is fewer notes but more action.

STOP (What do you need to stop doing?)

1.
2.
3.
4.
5.
6.

GROW (What new ways of doing things do you want to begin and how?)

1.
2.
3.
4.
5.
6.

FLOW (These are your ideas for making good practices a lifelong habit)

1.
2.
3.
4.
5.
6.

PART 3
ZOOM
BOOST! Your Skills

14 | START

Discover the secrets of sustaining your performance

Time is at once the most valuable and the most perishable of all our possessions

JOHN RANDOLPH

Don't start here

If you turned to this chapter first because it looks like it's about time management, you just made a big mistake. It's an understandable mistake to make. Time management is often high on the list when it comes to help at work. You may feel almost desperate for some tips and techniques and I will give you plenty, but first please make a *Big Mental Note* of this. Time management techniques alone will not fix your time management problem. It's like moving deck chairs on the Titanic when you're about to hit an iceberg. A waste of time.

I have read many specialist books about time management and many more that have included it as a chapter. You've probably read some of them too. Almost always there are missing ingredients that make it practically impossible to successfully apply the systems and ideas over the long term.

You go on a training course. You turn over a new leaf. You begin to apply the methods, but once again life crowds in, circumstances change and you find yourself going back to your old bad habits. Why? I know at least some of the critical reasons why this happens and what you can do about it.

Surprisingly, the factors that drive you back to your bad habits are not usually to do with your ability to follow time management tips. They are far more often to do with managing yourself and managing your interactions and relationships with others. That's why I wrote Parts One and Two. You are a whole person.

Climate control

You live in your own microclimate. It needs resources, balance and care if it's going to be sustainable. My mission is to help you make your working life, enterprise or cause easier, more successful and more enjoyable. I have noticed how the attempts of people to succeed in work, advance their careers, deal with change, cope with big workloads, manage their time, deliver projects, work successfully with others and build teams frequently falter because they are not giving the right kind of attention or taking action in all the areas that matter.

Your life is an ecosystem. It's like a machine – there have to be some fundamental elements in place or it isn't going to keep moving. I once made a long and ultimately very expensive journey. It was great fun at the time. Zooming down the motorway, music turned up loud. So loud I couldn't hear the dreadful noises coming from the engine. I discovered a little too late the oil warning light wasn't working. The engine had run dry and burnt out. That's what happens if you don't look after the system.

Three things must be in balance.

Firstly, clarity about your purpose and goals will enable you to fulfil your ambitions rather than letting the demands of others fill the vacuum. If you haven't worked out your own plan, someone will impose his or her plan on you. Secondly, becoming expert at influencing and bringing out the best in others will mean that you have the pleasure of achieving more and getting things done more easily. If you don't know how to push back and establish priorities and deadlines you'll be run into the ground. Lastly, you need to work hard on all the skills you need to be consistently excellent and more successful.

Successful time management requires you to pay attention to all the dimensions of your world. It can't be done in isolation. Work on your values, purpose, goals, focus, emotions and energy. Develop expertise in a whole mixture of supporting skills such as influencing, planning, managing your manager, problem solving and communicating. It's the combination of these things that will make it all work for you.

More with less

Organisations are reducing headcount and locking down recruitment at the same time. Sometimes your job description can double overnight. Administrative support is a thing of the past and the demands on your time seem to multiply on a daily basis. More and more is being asked of fewer people with the expectation of even greater performance. Keeping your business moving forward requires more knowledge, time and expertise. The possibilities are endless and the challenges increasing. Competition is fiercer, but resources are scarcer.

Added to this, the flow of information has increased astronomically, the expected speed of response has risen to an unsustainable pace and stress levels jump accordingly. Whatever your business, whether you own it or you are working in a bigger organisation, the pressures seem huge and at times insurmountable.

You may feel constantly tired and worn down, often dissatisfied with the amount of work you complete and the quality of work you do. Projects remain unfinished and you fear that those around you are let down by your failure to give them the quality time they need. All the time, you feel like you've never tried or worked harder.

You will have developed some coping mechanisms and some of them will be working. However, not all the habits you've developed will be helping you to reduce stress, increase fulfilment and get more done, more easily, more often. You know you could be so much more productive, achieving more, making more money and fulfilling more of your goals. Remember, though, this isn't about working harder, faster and longer. That doesn't make you more productive.

How does it all feel? Use the checklist to review how you are dealing with the pressures.

The Test of Time

Just tick the box (mentally at least) for each of these that apply to you.

1. I am constantly checking my email through the day ☐
2. I am often running late for meetings or appointments ☐
3. I constantly feel behind with my email ☐
4. I always answer the phone when it rings ☐
5. I find myself flitting between projects ☐
6. I tend to use my email inbox as my to do list ☐
7. I am constantly interrupted ☐
8. I struggle to focus on bigger projects ☐
9. I often leave the office feeling unfulfilled ☐
10. I feel behind with my work ☐
11. I worry that I am not getting enough done ☐
12. I have a lot of unfinished projects ☐
13. I feel my relationships suffer because of time pressure ☐
14. Sometimes I don't know what to do next ☐
15. I give little time to planning ☐
16. I'm not doing the most important things for my success ☐
17. I'm not getting enough exercise ☐
18. I have trouble sleeping ☐
19. I feel overwhelmed ☐
20. I take work home regularly ☐

Total _____

You'll know from your total what level of challenge you have. What can you do about it?

Start here

'Why does your job exist?'

I don't mean what is your job title or even your job description. I mean what is your job really supposed to achieve? Job descriptions are often amorphous and wide ranging and can easily lead to a focus on output rather than outcomes. You have to define it and translate it into your time use. What difference is your role supposed to make? Follow these steps to bring laser-like sharpness to your answer. Without this level of clarity you'll continue to be controlled by the problems described in the test above.

1. Describe your job under 5 main headings. Let's call these your Significant Achievement Areas. (SAA)
2. Against each of these, write a few bullet points that describe what success in those areas would look like. Let's call these your Significant Area Results. (SAR)
3. Make sure your diary and use of time match what you have written down
4. Stop doing *everything* that doesn't match! Success lies as much in knowing what you shouldn't do as what you must.
5. Don't ask your boss; often they have as little clarity as you. You should be the expert in your role. You should tell them what is most important, not the other way round.

It will take some time and thought, but it can make an incredible difference to your life. Imagine if your score for the Test of Time was low because all those useless and draining incidents weren't happening.

If you do this you will:

- Release your time to achieve the things you should be achieving
- Increase your sense of achievement
- Deliver more value and improved results for yourself and others
- Go home earlier
- Get noticed for achieving the right things
- Increase your self-esteem
- Be happier
- Have more free time
- Delight your customers (internal and external)
- Waste less time

Two into one doesn't go

You won't benefit from this if:

1. You don't apply it together with the rest of the advice about boosting yourself and your relationships

2. You are not courageous and radical. You may need to break bad habits that you might have been practising for years or even decades.

Are you ready to do something different? Good, because it is time to take control of your diary. Many people I have worked with don't know when to do their work, the SAAs. The reason is they feel they almost have two jobs: Job 1 and Job 2.

Job 1 constitutes *delivery*. This comprises the major and minor and everything in between pieces of work that you have to do to deliver on your SAAs. The papers, reports, analysis, meetings and projects you have to do to produce the results by which your success or otherwise is measured.

Job 2 is about *maintenance*. It involves handling the flow of communication (emails, calls, texts and social media), attending meetings with one or more people to review, update and discuss or present.

Of course, there is an overlap. Some of those meetings, emails, conversations and interruptions will be about your projects. The fact remains that you have to put in time to collate, think, write, plan, research and complete the work to produce the end product.

The problem is, Job 2 shouts the loudest. Job 2 can be so ravenous for your time that it completely consumes it and you are left with little, if any, time to do the real work of Job 1. It is the most persistent, the most habit forming, the easiest to focus on, and the most immediately gratifying. The computer says 'beep – do me now!' The Crackberry says 'beep – do me now!' It literally gives you a buzz. Tests show your response is exactly like the buzz from taking drugs.

Out with the old in with the new

The methods that follow will give you two fundamental skills for bringing your use of time into line with your SAAs. This will take a determined and consistent effort and the benefits can be massive. As beneficial as it is, it's still easier to continue working as you always have. You are likely to be working in an environment that has lots of bad practice so you will be paddling against the current. You'll need masses of motivation to change. Take a look back at Chapter 6. You'll need stacks of ZIP!

Using an electronic diary makes applying these models so much easier. The flexibility and colour coding that the technology gives you can help you stay organised, but remain flexible and you can have it with you all the time. The first method is so simple, but so important. The second is a fresh look at a classic model.

SKILL 1: MAKE APPOINTMENTS WITH YOURSELF
Most of you would be pretty disappointed if you called a meeting and no one showed up except for you. But believe me, these are going to be the best meetings of your week. Call a meeting, but only tell one person about it: you (don't forget to buy the biscuits).

Me-tings
STEP 1: Review your SAAs (Significant Achievement Areas) and the SARs (Significant Area Results) that if delivered successfully will demonstrate success.

STEP 2: Allocate time in your diary (I recommend one-hour or two-hour blocks) for the project work, thinking time, planning time, report writing, analysis etc. that will enable you to complete your projects on time. Don't leave blanks in your diary for this. You or others will fill them.

STEP 3: Plan as far ahead as you can. Look ahead and plan the time across the period you have to complete the projects. Estimate how much time it will take. If you estimate 10 hours and you have a five-week deadline allocate two hours per week. If there aren't obvious deadlines, create your own. Recurrent meetings should follow the same pattern with the appropriate preparation and follow up time scheduled around them.

STEP 4: If someone asks for a meeting or call during a 'me-ting' your answer is that you are busy. If it is a request you must agree to then move your 'me-ting' to another slot in your diary. Do not delete it.

SKILL 2: PRIORITISING

I recently read a well-known time management book about how to get things done without too much effort. In it, the author refers to the familiar Important-Urgent matrix for time management. I have used this matrix many times as I think it is a very useful basis for helping people to learn to prioritise. Unfortunately, the writer has misrepresented how to use the tool and therefore nullifies its effectiveness. He recommends concentrating on 1 and 3; this is wrong, as it means you will be constantly running around dealing with the urgent, whether it is important or not. The best use of this matrix is frequently misrepresented so here's your chance to learn to use it correctly.

Important – Urgent

This tool is frequently misunderstood, misused or unused, but it is still one of the most practical and easy ways to take control of your use of time. Here are seven simple stages to understand, use and master the Important-Urgent matrix.

1. Important and Urgent	2. Important but Not Urgent
3. Not Important but Urgent	4. Not Important and Not Urgent

1. Fill in the boxes from your current 'To do' list. (You do have a 'To do' list, don't you?) Decide into which box each item falls.
2. If you have too many items in the Important and Urgent box (Box 1) you are fire-fighting; this will increase stress and working hours, but reduce quality of relationships and quality of work. There will always be things in Box 1, but they should be the exception not the rule.
3. All the time you have an overwhelming number of items in Box 1 you will not get around to the Important but Not Urgent items (Box 2), ever or until they too become urgent and move over to Box 1, thus compounding your problems.

4. The Important but Not Urgent box (Box 2) includes items such as: Major projects and initiatives, Key objectives, Developing self and others, Longer term planning, Team time, Relationship building, Thinking, Reviewing, Appraisals, Delegating, Education, Rest, Innovation. All your SAAs and SARs appear here.
5. Work out what is Important for you to be doing and concentrate your efforts here (Box 2). These are the results that are fundamental to your work. The more time you spend in Box 2 the more you will reduce what builds up in Box 1.
6. Create more time to concentrate on Box 2 by *eliminating* Box 3 and Box 4 activities. No one has yet been able to tell me something that is Not Important but Urgent (Box 3) that they really must do. It is usually someone else's crisis. If it is important for your relationship that you help them, it is Box 1. Encourage them to plan better next time or say 'No'.
7. Box 4 equals the time wasting activities such as interruptions, unproductive meetings, some emails, some calls etc. Cut them out.

Mastering these skills and thinking with this precision is a life skill that saves masses of time that would be wasted, reduces stress and enables you to produce the important results. It will reduce your hours in the office and your time spent on work away from the office. You'll also need to be aware of all the time-stealers that can derail you, leaving your plans in tatters. You've read about some of the critical skills already in PUSH and SWERVE. Keep reading for even more.

BIG MENTAL NOTE

Time management techniques alone will not fix your time management problem.

| ONE SMALL STEP |

Start having Me-tings (don't forget the biscuits).

15 | STOP

Become time-rich

Time is the most valuable thing a man can spend
THEOPHRASTUS

Money and time

Time is a precious commodity. It doesn't come back. You can't go and get more from anywhere. Successful people don't waste time. Parting a successful person from their time is like trying to part a rich person from his or her money. If you treat money like time is often treated, you'd be in a really sticky situation. Money runs out, and it can lead to terrible consequences. It's the same with time. So why do you give away your time so easily?

Brian Tracy says that the most successful people are the best procrastinators. How come? You thought procrastination was a bad thing, didn't you? What he means is that successful people put off the things that are not going to help their mission or fulfil their goals. Then they put them off again. Eventually they just fall off the list altogether. Sometimes this is a difficult thing to predict, but many things that people tell you are urgent are gradually dropped and never heard of again.

Don't just jump when they say jump.

You might think that if you only had more time everything would be okay. How much more time do you think you might need? Another three hours a day; another four; who'll give me five? If you did have another five hours per day, what do you think might happen in about a year from now? Yes, that's right, you'd need more. Very few jobs are simply nine to five. The demands made on you frequently seem unreasonable. That's why you have to learn to be expert at controlling your use of time by using all the ideas in this book.

Like money, it is better to budget time and decide where it's going, rather than not budget and ask where it has gone.

Budget time

Before we go any further, let me ask you, 'Do you actually know where your time is going?' When I was first married I couldn't understand why, when two salaries were coming in and it was just two to keep fed and sheltered, we still went overdrawn every month. The problem with going overdrawn is you always feel behind. You always feel at a disadvantage and it has a knock-on effect and things get worse. It's hard to catch up.

Something needed to change.

The first book I read about managing money taught me how to take control of my budgeting. One of the first things it prescribed was making a note of everything that you spent. I mean everything. If I spent £5 each day on a newspaper, parking and chewing gum, items like these totalled £150 per month. Day by day, for a month, I made a note of everything I spent. Do you know what I discovered: I was spending my money on all sorts of things I hadn't budgeted for. What a revelation! I didn't realise where my money was going. It wasn't that I didn't have enough money for my needs; the problem was I was wasting my money without realising it.

When I added all these irregular expenditures to the regular outgoings, I could see why I was overdrawn every month. What was the solution? Budget for everything. Put money aside for *all* your needs. Don't just hope it will be all right in the end. I have frequently noticed that people who have never wanted for money don't need to budget much. If you've got plenty of it, why restrict it. But if you are hard up, you better budget because you'll be in big trouble if you don't.

How much time did you say you had? Are you stretched? Better do some time budgeting!

STOP | 133

Track your time

Everyone loves a spreadsheet, don't they?

Not in my world, and I doubt whether you would fill it in even if it was printed right here. In order to find out where your time is going you need to keep a record of it. For at least three days – one week if you can –, keep a diary of where your time is going. Just like I did for my money diet: note down everything. The easiest way to do it is to create a table with time slots and then devise a simple key for the activities e – e-mail, t – telephone, m – meeting, SAA 1, SAR 1. You'll need a bit more detail because you must know on what and to whom the time is going. Who knows, a spreadsheet might work for you!

Once you've completed it, look at where your time is going. Here are some questions to consider.

- How much of your time is being eaten away by maintenance (Job 2)?
- How much of your time is spent on the real work (Job 1)?
- Who is taking your time?
- What percentage of your time is being used by each activity?
- What does this tell you about your use of time?
- What could you change so that you improve the balance?

Catch the time thieves

There are activities, people and incidents that creep into your day, and have become the norm, that are making you unproductive and inefficient. The next section smashes five of the most common time stealers and gives you ways of dealing with them. Remember, stealing your time is just like someone stealing your money. Time is money and time is also the currency of relaxation, concentration, effectiveness, pleasure, fulfilment and stress reduction. When you lose your time or fragment your time it has an impact on all these things.

TIME THIEF 1: EMAIL
Almost everyone I know seems to be a slave to his or her inbox. Some wear it as a badge of honour. "I had 79 emails waiting for me when I got back from lunch!" (Not that they would be the type to go to

lunch!) Mostly, people are drowning in it. It plays to your sense of self worth and you feel insecure when you are not getting the hits regularly, every few moments. There's useful email and useless email.

This isn't easy to fix because most of the bad practice will come from your boss, your customers and other significant people. You may not be able to cure others, but that's no excuse for spreading the germs. It can be significantly improved and here are some of the things you should do.

Six tips for taking control of your inbox and reducing useless email:
1. Learn how to write them.
   - ✓ Use the subject line to specifically describe the purpose and response time needed
   - ✓ Write it like a news story. The most important info is at the beginning not the end
   - ✓ Keep it short
   - ✓ Don't be lazy: don't send people large attachments without explaining the significance or, better still, which parts are most relevant.
   - ✓ Don't copy others in on huge email trails unnecessarily or without doing the same as the one above.

2. Pick up the telephone instead. Leave or send voice messages if necessary.
3. Stop responding instantly and have set times of the day when you will review your email. Let others know when you do this. There is no possible way that everything that comes into your inbox is urgent. What does urgent mean? It must be done now. If the email says, 'Dear Sir or Madam, The building is on fire, leave now, Kind regards, The Fire Brigade' that is urgent! Deal with that straightaway.
4. You cannot deal with everything all the time.
5. Stop using your email as your 'To do' list. Use the tools in the previous chapter to ensure effective use of your time.
6. If people send you badly written emails without subjects or deadlines call them and ask for clarification. Change their behaviour.

TIME THIEF 2: PROCRASTINATION

Why do you not do things that you know you need to get on and do?

For all of the examples below, see yourself successfully completing each step rather than the whole thing, and then do each one. For example, if you know you should go to the gym today and you even want to go to the gym but can't seem to do it, first see yourself completing each step and then do them one by one.

- Get your kit together
- Go to the gym
- Get changed
- Warm up
- Start your workout

Four reasons why you don't get on with things and what to do about it:

Reason 1. It's too big
The task in front of you seems overwhelming and you don't know where to start.

Solution 1:
   ✓ Say to yourself, 'I'll just spend a few minutes on this.' Often you'll keep going, but whatever happens you'll make a start.
   ✓ Start to break it down into bits. Use a mind map as an easy way to put the whole thing on one page

Reason 2. It's too hard
Often you feel you don't know how to do something.

Solution 2:
   ✓ Ask yourself what you've done before that has been similar and use that knowledge to help you get going
   ✓ Without editing/questioning yourself, write down possible ways to do it
   ✓ Ask for help

Reason 3. It's too scary
You put off work or conversations because they are sensitive, awkward or tricky and may have unpredictable outcomes.

Solution 3:
- ✓ Make a plan. What's a desirable outcome?
- ✓ Consider what could work for or against the desired outcome
- ✓ Develop ideas to build on what will work for it and manage what could work against it
- ✓ If the challenge involves others, work through each step considering their viewpoint as well
- ✓ Implement the plan

Reason 4. It's too small:
It's easy to keep putting off insignificant but important tasks; then they become urgent and big.

Solution 4:
- ✓ Just do it. Put it in your diary, even if it should only take 5 minutes
- ✓ Tell someone else you are going to do it and ask them to check up
- ✓ Do it with someone else
- ✓ Group a number of small but similar things together and get them done as quickly as you can. Set yourself a challenge and give yourself a reward

TIME THIEF 3: INTERRUPTIONS AND DIVERSIONS
Everything, from the distractions of open-plan offices to email alerts, the internet, the telephone, your dog and small children, will tempt you away from the important.

What to do?

Five rules for keeping control
1. If it is urgent and important, **Do it** as soon as you can
2. If it is important but not urgent **Decide when** to do it. Make a note in your diary or to do list now.
3. If it is urgent but not important for *you* to do, either **Delegate it, Push back or Ignore** (it will probably go away)
4. If it is neither urgent nor important, **Dump it**.
5. See Part Two for how to successfully work with people in these different scenarios. Especially chapter 10.

STOP | 137

TIME THIEF 4: MEETINGS

Meetings, a bit like email, tend to be one of those crutches you can lean on to reassure yourself that you are important and valuable. If you are invited to a meeting it may give you a little lift. They also eat a huge amount of your time so they had better be worth it.

Eight Question Meeting Evaluator

- Q1. What is the purpose of the meeting?
- Q2. What's the value of the meeting for your SAAs and SARs?
- Q3. What's the agenda?
- Q4. What's the length of the meeting?
- Q5. What's my contribution?
- Q6. Do I need to attend all/any of it?
- Q7. Could I make my contribution in another way?
- Q8. Could it be a development opportunity for someone else?

Make your brain brilliant

Multi-tasking is probably the prime cause of inefficiency, time poverty and increased stress among knowledge and idea workers. Whoever put it into your head that if you flit from task to task, first focusing on one thing and then on another and then back to the one before, it would make you more productive? It doesn't.

Monotask

We've already looked at a number of ideas to help with this. Focus and concentration are the keys and it's difficult because you've been training your brain to jump around ceaselessly. Now you need to train it back. How?

- ✓ Do one thing at a time
- ✓ Finish tasks, or the portion of the task you've decided to do, before moving on to the next thing
- ✓ Choose when: what's your best time of day to do the work that needs the most concentration?
- ✓ Choose where: in conversation with one client who struggled with this, he said that often his most productive place was on train journeys. I suggested he buy a return ticket for

somewhere that gave him the right amount of time to get things done. Be radical – break the habit.
- ✓ Choose what: it's unusual not to have a number of key things going on at the same time. This means you have to be adept at spinning a number of plates concurrently. If a chef only did one thing at a time, she'd have some pretty boring, cold food and unhappy customers.

There are two secrets to success:

- ✓ Secret 1: Focus on the few. Decide which significant things have to be worked on concurrently
- ✓ Secret 2: Filter all other interruptions. Don't drift into general multi-tasking.

Research shows that the multi-tasking habits you have adopted make you 30 percent less productive, make you more anxious and stressed, and create addictive behaviour. Yes, 30 percent. What could you do with an extra 1.5 days each week? I've got an idea. Do more planning.

BIG MENTAL NOTE

It is better to budget time, like money, and decide where it's going, rather than not budget and ask where it has gone.

| ONE SMALL STEP |

Develop the mono-tasking mentality.

16 | PLAN

Create your course for certain super-productivity

Our goals can only be reached through a vehicle of a plan, in which we must fervently believe, and upon which we must vigorously act. There is no other route to success.

PABLO PICASSO

Ferry stressful

Pablo Picasso was an enormously creative, spontaneous and imaginative man, but he still had a plan. My friend Tom isn't the most natural planner. One memorable year he left all the extra bits of shopping he needed to do for the family holiday until quite late the day before they left. Not a problem in itself; not until the unexpected occurred. At this point, he was feeling fairly organised maybe even a little proud of himself. After all, he'd allocated a whole day to make sure they had the final provisions needed before they set off by car to catch the ferry to France early in the morning on the next day. They hadn't had a family holiday for a couple of years so Tom's wife, Julie, and the boys were really excited about the trip.

He walked into town with his list and visited lots of shops to gather the last important things. Feeling very pleased with himself he set off home as the shops were closing. They live in a very friendly neighbourhood with a thriving community and often have the front door unlocked. He walked straight into his house and he and his wife continued packing the clothes, shoes, food, swimming gear, towels and books and all the other paraphernalia you need for your family holiday.

So far, so good...

As the evening wore on, and the packing was nearly complete, they thought they'd start to put a few things into the car so they'd be able to get away quicker the next day. But where were the keys? They only had one set of car keys. They began to hunt for the keys, but they were nowhere to be found. They must have been packed. So they began the tortuous task of unpacking all the bags. Out came the swimming costumes, food, books, shoes and so on and so on. No keys. You know how it is – you then go through everywhere you've just looked again and again. No keys. Then you retrace what you've done since you got home and look everywhere else. They turned the place upside down. No keys.

You can imagine that tempers were getting frayed by now.

Tom's wife asked, 'So how did you get in the house when you came back from the shops?'

'The door was open', says Tom. That's when it struck them. Tom must have left their only set of car keys in one of the shops he'd visited that day. But now it's late and all the shops are closed. How would they ever get away on their holiday? I'll tell you at the end of the chapter...

Push me pull you

In the original *Doctor Doolittle* children's books by Hugh Lofting, there's an animal called the *pushmi-pullyu*. It's a cross between a gazelle and a unicorn and it has two heads, one at each end. When it tries to move, both heads go in opposite directions. This is like our relationship with planning. It's a bit of a love-hate relationship. Even when you try to do it you may not be very skilled, just like Tom. Logically, you know that it's a good thing to plan, but everything about your fragmented and time-pressured life seems to pull you in the opposite direction. It's a conundrum.

I'll be bold. I think I know at least some of the main reasons you don't plan. Feel free to correct me and add your own.

× Planning takes too long

PLAN | 141

- ✗ Planning processes seem over-complicated
- ✗ Plans don't work out as you expect
- ✗ You don't have time
- ✗ You don't know how to
- ✗ Life moves too fast
- ✗ Plans aren't flexible enough
- ✗ People and plans don't mix
- ✗ You'd rather get on with work than think about it
- ✗ It feels like a waste of time
- ✗ It's boring!

But if I asked you what the benefits of planning are, you might come up with ideas like:

- ✓ Helps everyone pull together
- ✓ Helps everyone stay on course
- ✓ Helps you plan your own and others' workload
- ✓ Makes sure you think about everything involved in a project
- ✓ Helps you to co-ordinate resources
- ✓ More of the right things happen at the right time
- ✓ Helps with communication
- ✓ Helps you allocate your time
- ✓ It saves time
- ✓ It avoids false starts (going back to the drawing board)
- ✓ It can save costly oversights
- ✓ May avert disaster

So maybe what you need is a planning model that is quick, easy, flexible, simple, people-friendly and fun. Can such a thing possibly exist? Give these ideas a try and let me know. Follow these steps for a 15-minute planning process.

Think purpose not process

If you are a fully functioning, project management software user or have every project planning certification there is, you could still find this useful. The best and quickest way to get your planning fired up is by thinking about what you want to achieve. Stephen Covey says, 'Start with the end in mind.' Planning can seem like such a hassle because the process takes all our energy, when what you really need is a purpose that you are excited about. Otherwise it is dry and boring. Focus first on what will be the reward for all your time and effort. First, get an exciting and motivating purpose and then work on the process.

15-minute planning
There are five steps so you have three minutes for each. I know you'll want to go back to some and put in more detail for bigger tasks, but you'll be amazed how helpful 15-minute planning can be. Especially when compared to zero-minute planning. There are two tricks for doing this in three minutes per step.

1. Ask someone else to work through this with you. All they have to do is ask you the questions and keep you on track following the process.
2. Don't second-guess yourself. When you think of something, write it down. Don't question. You need pace not perfection.

I've seen many people get a breakthrough for kick-starting major pieces of work and projects in less than 15 minutes using this process, especially when they have the help of a colleague, but you can do it by yourself. It crushes procrastination.

STEP 1: VISION
What result or outcome do you really want? What would be a great result? The first step in your simple planning process is *defining your Vision*. It might sound a bit grand for your project, but in simple terms it is an inspiring picture of a desired future. Motivation is as important in your planning process as it is in achieving any kind of change. Ask yourself questions as if you'd already achieved the result:

- ✓ What does a good job look like?
- ✓ What are you proud to have achieved?
- ✓ Who are my customers now?
- ✓ What great things are they saying about me?
- ✓ What's improved because of what I've achieved?

When you do this, you need to project yourself into the future and think about what you will have, *as if* you've completed the plan. Don't get hung up on that, but it is a neat little trick that requires you to spice up the process with extra doses of confidence.

STEP 2: REALITY

One of the main reasons plans go awry is you haven't thought of what could throw it off course. It's too easy to get precious about your plan. People are often singularly unpredictable and disobliging compared to our lovely neat plan. They won't always respond to fit in with your timetable in the way you want.

You may have heard of SWOT: not a new fly spray but a simple method to weigh up a situation and then create options.

It helps you ask, and answer, the following questions. If you are working with a team then you simply pluralise everything. (Replace 'my' with 'our'.)

- ✓ Which of my **S**trengths will help achieve the vision?
- ✓ Which of my **W**eaknesses could hinder achieving the vision?
- ✓ What **O**pportunities are there that could help achieve the vision?
- ✓ What **T**hreats exist that could hinder achieving the vision?

Remember, this is a quick process so you are not trying to create endless lists. Try to focus quickly on the main topics for each. Just a couple of bullet points will do.

The first two are about you, your team or organisation (Internal).

The others are about what's going on around you: outside you, your team and organisation (External). If you are looking at internal change, then the 'external' part may be within your organisation as well.

STEP 3: OPTIONS

Now it's time for you to create some options. The important point here is to create options for achieving your vision using the insights you've had answering the SWOT questions.

To do this, you match external opportunities and threats with your internal strengths and weaknesses.

Create options under each of these headings:

- ✓ Options which use your strengths to maximise the opportunities
- ✓ Options which use your strengths to avoid or manage the threats
- ✓ Options which minimize your weaknesses by taking advantage of opportunities
- ✓ Options which minimize your weaknesses and avoid or manage threats

Remember, this is a quick process so you are not trying to create endless lists. Try to focus quickly on the main topics for each. Just a couple of bullet points will do.

STEP 4: MILESTONES

From your options, you can now choose your timeframes and what needs to be done when. Too often people jump to this stage straight away and then wonder why things don't go according to plan. Your options may include things like working out and securing a budget, resources needed, getting sponsors on board, consulting with other stakeholders and communication plans.

Simply work out what needs to happen in the **short, medium and long term.** If the project needs to be complete within six months, break up the timeframe accordingly and slot in the tasks you've selected. Keep your plan under review. Remember, tasks almost always take longer than you expect. You'll have a tendency to underestimate what needs to be done and overestimate your ability to get it done. A deadly mix.

STEP 5: ACTION

The final part of the plan is to assign the tasks to people. If it is just for you then make Me-tings in your diary throughout the project period until completion. Decide when and what you are going to do with whom. If others are involved, the more who are involved in this whole process the better.

How to be a robot

This may not appear to be the most appealing idea in the book until you understand what it means. Robot stands for Right On Budget On Time. It's not a bad reputation to have because most people deliver exactly the opposite. Sadly, it's often accepted that's just the way it is. People go into countless meetings unprepared and expecting everything to be served up on a plate.

You can stand out for the right reasons. You can use this process to quickly get a clear idea of the outcomes you want to achieve. Successful meetings, for example, are not the ones that cover the agenda. They are the ones when you get the outcomes you are focused on. You can plan your way to success 15 minutes at a time.

You can use that process to quickly plan a telephone call or a meeting to make them more productive. If you think with this kind of structure you will set yourself apart as someone with insight and intelligence and you'll be ahead of the pack. The message is plan quickly and constantly. You'll train your brain to be more efficient and effective in no time at all and you'll have more success quicker with what you want to achieve.

Tom and Julie's holiday

Now Tom may not be the best planner, but he is resourceful. He remembered as well as he could the shops he'd visited and went back in the dead of night and posted notes through every letterbox. The note explained his plight, gave his number and asked them to look for the keys. At 8 a.m. the next morning (and no sleep) his cell phone rang. Yes! Someone had found the keys. He got a taxi to the shop and back, packed in double quick time and two hours later they all caught the ferry by the skin of their teeth. No problem.

Imagine what an impact you can make if you can be incredibly smart at planning *and* resourceful. Careers flatten out then nosedive if you rely too heavily only on the capabilities and skills that got you to where you are today. You must be continually learning and growing as an individual and as a business or you'll be obsolete before you know it. Don't expect to sit still and make progress. You'll just become a couch potato. Lasting success is for the growers, the learners and the tryers. Alvin Toffler wrote, 'the illiterate of the 21st century will be those who cannot learn, unlearn and relearn.'

BIG MENTAL NOTE

First, get an exciting and motivating purpose and then work on the process.

| ONE SMALL STEP |

Practise this process with a colleague. You help them then they help you. Choose something you each need to get more organised about. Not too big – it's just practice.

---

17 | ACHIEVE

Make an unforgettable positive impact

It's not enough to be busy. The question is 'What are you busy about?'

DAVID HENRY THOREAU

Is there anybody there?

In an episode of the *Friends* comedy series (about a group of single people living together in an apartment in Manhattan), Phoebe starts a telemarketing job at an office supplies company. She has to call people to sell toner. She calls a depressed customer called Earl whose reason for not needing toner is that he is going to kill himself that very day. He even has it written on his to do list. There isn't a reply in her telephone script for that one. He complains that after 10 years no one even knows that he exists. In fact, to prove it, he shouts out to the others in the office that he's going to kill himself and he gets no response whatsoever. It is funny – promise.

Earl has been in the job for 10 years and no one knows that he exists. Someone once asked me a very provocative question. 'If you weren't here would anyone notice?' It sounds like a mean question. Of course it's not meant in a personal way. People would miss you as a person, but would they miss what you've been achieving? It's a question you should be asking yourself on a regular basis before other people start asking it about you.

Busyness is not a measure of success

It is too easy to get into the routine of fulfilling a role. The various relationships, rhythms and challenges go on from one month to the next.

You attend the meetings, complete the tasks and do the updates. You do your best to keep everything moving and deliver your objectives. You dial into the conference calls and keep in touch with the clients. You are busy, very busy, even giving up personal time to keep the wheels turning, but are you making a difference to anything? This all adds up to one thing. It's easily forgotten.

Recently I was involved with an organisation going through significant restructuring. Many people had to reapply for jobs or apply for new roles internally. The process was heavily evidence-based. As a result, I was involved helping people to prepare for this challenge. Sometimes it is not until you have to write down your achievements in a CV that you think this way. The rest of the time you can so easily focus on busyness and the challenges of busyness and workload that you forget to ask fundamental questions.

- What are you actually achieving?
- What achievements could you write down if you had to apply for your own job today?
- What do you have to write down that is relevant to what your job and organisation will look like next year and the year after?
- What can you point to in terms of your impact on tangible achievements?

Busyness becomes the focus because it's easier than asking yourself the uncomfortable questions. Although it doesn't feel that way at the time.

Even if you have agreed your objectives with your manager, don't be complacent. Results are what matter in the end. They matter for you. I know you can argue that you are doing what is required and that you'll get a good appraisal. But you have to be more engaged with your own career than your manager or organisation. Why? Your fulfilment, satisfaction and future is too important to leave in the hands of others, however well meaning. They won't be thinking about what could be coming around the corner before it's too late. You have to be hyper-engaged with your own purpose and passions and performance.

Rewrite those objectives until they can be quantified and you can prove to anyone how you deliver value. Look at what you are doing and how can you directly link it to tangible improvements in terms of quality, quantity or condition for your customers and company. If you can't sit down today and add things to your CV or professional social profile you can be proud of – then beware. You could be falling into the trap of fulfilling a busy function without delivering vital concrete results. Every day you should be thinking of the next stage of satisfaction and reward you want, and what you need to do to get it. Your job is unlikely to last forever, or even as long as you want it to. It's unlikely to be fulfilling forever.

Think about yourself as if you are a business that must keep ahead of the competition. If you own a shop, for example, but you don't have customers you are in trouble. But having customers is not enough. These customers must be delighted, shopping regularly, telling their friends, which in turn brings in more cash, allowing you to invest in the range of products and improve your services, employ more staff and keep ahead of the competition. What happens when you stand still? The rest of the world moves on.

The Frog and Ostrich

No, not the name of my local pub.

There's a well-known story that if you put a frog in water and heat it slowly enough it won't jump out, but will gradually boil, but if you tried to toss it into a pan of boiling water it would jump out. The ostrich also gets a bad press. Supposedly it buries its head in the sand when danger is coming.

These two hypothetical metaphors are used to illustrate two real problems:

Problem 1: Frog – Disasters can creep up on you a bit at a time and that's why you don't change until it's too late.

Problem 2: Ostrich – Rather than face the facts of impending problems you prefer to ignore or deny them in the hope that they'll go away. Also a risky strategy.

Taking notice of these ideas won't make you bulletproof in your job. That's not the point. The point is that every moment of every day you are fanatical about your enterprise as if it is your own business and your own money at stake. Your mentality is to be a world-beater at what you love doing. If this role stopped, it wouldn't matter because you will have already thought well ahead. In fact, when this role disappears it won't matter because you will have already moved on. If you haven't, you'll know why and you'll already have your plan for the next stage of your mission.

Shoot for the stars don't howl at the moon

Things don't just change by themselves. Some events may seem to happen by magic, but even these require the right conditions. Trees bud, flowers blossom and grass grows. Crops replenish, young birds hatch and kids get bigger. Behind the scenes feeding, watering, propagating, breeding, sheltering and cultivating all play their part in creating the magic. You soon start to notice when these things are absent or breakdown.

If you want the results you have to take action.

You have to be the kind of person who thinks about creating solutions rather than adding to the problem. If you are a 'shoot' rather than a 'howl' kind of person, you are thinking about the concrete steps that can be taken to make a positive difference rather than all the reasons why something cannot be changed. Instead of endlessly discussing all the ins and outs, you are more interested in discussing options. Instead of waiting for others, you constantly think about how to get things moving and do something about it. Instead of seeing the negative and insurmountable, you see the positive and possible.

Remember, achieving is often nothing to do with what has been written on your job specification. Job specifications tend to be written by the sort of people who mistake activity for achievements. This means you have to be a self-starter, a problem-solver and a counter-cultural thinker and doer. You are not there to fill the hours of the day looking busy until you can get away as early as possible to make it to the weekend when you can really live. If you are doing something that interests, challenges and motivates you, you are there to make a difference. If you are not interested, challenged and motivated then you are in the wrong place doing the wrong thing and you need to re-read Part One. You may have become stale and demotivated and even bored, but this could kick-start your rejuvenation, then who knows where you'll go.

Explore

People who deliver meaningful results are usually those who have a passion and a belief for what they do. They refuse to be ground down by the system. They find a way. They are always asking, 'How could we?' not 'Why can't we?' You can be one of those people. Instead of thinking what's not working, think about what is working and how you can do more of it. Look for the bright spots and work with those, even when the majority of the situation appears bleak.

You'll also become skilled at seeing opportunities for making things better than they are now. It's not simply about fixing things that have gone wrong, but taking the initiative to generate new ideas. Revive your curiosity and ask, 'What if?' Lift your head and notice the things that could be done better; make suggestions and play with options. Introduce some light-heartedness and derring-do. It will make life and work more fulfilling and fun. Who knows, you could do something extraordinary.

Analytical thinking

Before you can become an effective problem-solver you need to know a couple of things about thinking. It's useful to think in different ways at different times. As with many of the ideas I have given you, there is a simple way of implementing it.

Think in colour

Below are descriptions of two types of thinking which it is important for you to master. To get the best results from this method, remember not to mix the two, but use them at different stages of the C: D.R.I.V.E process that follows. Create first and edit later. If you edit while trying to create, the ideas will dry up.

- ✓ Green Thinking (GT): If you are in exploratory or creative mode then you need your thoughts to flow freely and without interruption because that's when you'll discover the most interesting things. This is called Green Thinking. Green in most cultures means 'Go'. It encourages progress and flow and forward motion. When you are using Green Thinking (GT) you are in Open mode.
- ✓ Red Thinking (RT): If you are evaluating options or deciding on the best course of action, use Red Thinking. Red Thinking provides the safety net for Green Thinking. You can be free to come up with all the ideas you want because you know you'll use Red Thinking to evaluate. Red in most cultures means stop and caution. It means wait and review. When you are using Red Thinking (RT) you are in Closed mode.

How to be a problem-solver

If you want to stand out as an opportunity-grabber and a problem-solver, you'll need a quick process to structure your thoughts and drive change. Many people make the mistake of too readily jumping to solutions. It's possible to come up with a great solution to the wrong problem. To begin with, you need to engage your critical and analytical thinking skills to avoid wasting time, money and goodwill. Combine these with understanding, asking, listening and persuading as described in previous chapters, and you'll become expert at delivering outstanding results. C: D.R.I.V.E blends all this together.

C: D.R.I.V.E

This model is designed to help you quickly focus on the relevant issue and create options for a way forward, and at the same time give attention to getting the right people onboard. The easiest way to describe this is for you to imagine yourself working with a group of colleagues or a customer or potential client. The normal place to start with any issue is the Context.

- ✓ **Context** – Let those who are closest to the problem describe in broad terms what is going on now
- ✓ **Data** – Collect all the relevant facts and group them into similar facts (GT). Make sure you distinguish between facts and assumptions (RT)
- ✓ **Reality** – In the light of the facts, define the real problem. When you hear the context you may think the problem or opportunity is one thing, but when you have considered the facts you will often discover it is another (RT)
- ✓ **Innovate** – Now brainstorm ideas for possible solutions. This is not the solution. These are possible solutions (GT)
- ✓ **Validate** – Decide on your criteria for deciding which, out of your possible solutions, is the best way forward (RT)
- ✓ **Engage** – In order for any solution to be implemented you need the involvement and support of the key people who'll be affected (See Chapter 18 about implementing change). It comes at the end of the word (DRIVE), but they need to be involved at the beginning of the process so that your efforts won't be wasted. Together you can develop the Action Plan which should be incorporated in the solution.

BIG MENTAL NOTE

'If you weren't here would anyone notice?' It's a question you should be asking yourself on a regular basis before other people start asking it about you.

| ONE SMALL STEP |

Find the bright spots in something that doesn't seem to be working. Discover what is working. Then make more bright spots happen.

18 | PLAY

Renew your joy and become one of the great explorers

Only those who risk going too far can possibly find out how far one can go.

T.S. ELLIOT

Discomfort zone

You are familiar with the phrase 'comfort zone', but how often do you venture into a discomfort zone. That's the zone where you try new things, take risks and confront the possibility of failure in order to grow. Failing is built into success. You can get frozen in your development because you think you have to be able to move from where you are to a more desirable place in one giant, error-free bound. Then you get frustrated at the first setbacks or you don't even bother to try because it seems too big. It's so frustrating when you feel you can't get there from here. But you can if you are prepared to fail.

First you'll have to stop expecting the best. Having a fixed idea that there is a 'best' or a fixed definition of success is one of the big reasons you may not move from where you are to where you want to go, and get the life you want. Perfection is for earthlings not explorers.

I worked with a personal trainer for a while and learned that the way to increase fitness and strength is to push to the point of failure. That's when you increase your strength, endurance and capacity. You break down muscles through the strain you put on them and then bigger, stronger muscles grow. You tend to prefer to stay within your comfort zone. Why is it called a comfort zone? That's the place where you are working within your limits. It's where you know exactly what you are doing. You don't need to learn anything or risk anything and all the outcomes are predictable.

You need to get into your discomfort zone. Not because someone made you, but because you want to grow.

Failure is success

If you hadn't started life as a failure, you'd still be shuffling around on your bottom. When you were learning to walk, doting parents cheered on each apparently drunken attempt. In your developing mind this game of standing up, weaving unsteadily across the room by making your legs move and then collapsing in a heap gave adults so much apparent fun that you just kept on doing it. In fact you kept on doing it so often that before long you found yourself upright more often than toppling over or crawling around like the cat, and this gave you new and unexpected opportunities.

It seemed like a big game. There were a few bumps and bruises to cope with, maybe even a few tears, but it was worth it. When you were learning to walk you were not expected to advance from relatively competent crawler to instant walker. It didn't happen like that. It was more like learning to un-crawl than learning to walk at first. You were cheered on and encouraged even when you made a complete mess of it. They didn't say, 'You've been trying this for three days now and you haven't got the hang of it so time's up. You'll just have to stay on the ground. Too bad.'

Perfect? Nonsense!

When does all that change? When do you get to the point when life becomes black and white and you start talking about failure and success as if they are two definable set points and you are either at one or the other? Your life and work are a journey filled with successes and failures and highs and lows. There is not a destination called retirement when you finally get to do what you've always wanted.

If you are over concerned with doing it right you'll put the brakes on adventure, creativity and imagination. It's not that you shouldn't be concerned about getting things right at the right time, like if you are landing an aeroplane, but don't let it squash your sense of fun. If your work itself isn't at times playful and fun then you run the risk that it will become unremittingly draining.

I worked with a project director who needed help keeping on top of his workload. His portfolio involved a number of multi-million projects and he had all manner of teams working for him. He was running himself into the ground because he constantly checked and double-checked every aspect of the work. During our conversation it emerged that he was also a keen carpenter. He told me how he had built a table for his home. He had spent well over 100 hours of his leisure time creating the perfect table and, even though everyone thought it was fantastic, he wasn't totally satisfied so he destroyed it.

Overworked and underjoyed

What's at the root of this sort of behaviour? In your background you may have parents or other authority figures who set very high standards for you and didn't forgive or understand mistakes. You might think that unless something is completely right you have failed, and that people will think less of you if you make a mistake. You may have had a boss who had a similar impact. The result is your ability to experiment, be curious and risk failing has been systematically erased.

I borrowed the subtitle above from Tim Ferris of *Four Hour Work Week* fame. It's usually the high achieving, highly capable types – who find it hard to know 'How good is good enough' who get trapped in a cycle of hard graft that allows no space for anything less than perfect. Often referred to as perfectionism, it has insidious and not always obvious ramifications.

When you start your career, you may have the time and space to perfect all your work assignments and make them the very best that they can be. After all, 'If a job is worth doing, it's worth doing well'. As you take on more responsibility, with a wider portfolio, more complex projects and others to oversee, you no longer have the time or capacity to work in the same way. That doesn't stop you trying to carry on as if nothing has changed.

Just as you can get referred pain because of a problem somewhere else in your body, being a perfectionist creates a number of referred problems for you, such as:

1. Working over long hours
2. Working at home in the evenings and weekends
3. Missed deadlines
4. Over-working pieces of work, only to have the specification changed by others
5. Not matching your time to your priorities
6. Over-emphasis on minor things as well as the major things
7. Imposing this working ethos on others through micromanagement
8. Losing sleep
9. Potential burnout
10. High stress levels

Some of the results of this will be obvious to you already. There can be tension at home because the laptop or mobile take your attention yet again. You live with guilt that you are not giving enough time to your personal life or your work life; with the uncomfortable tension in the pit of your stomach that nothing is ever good enough. Your health, sleep and fitness may be suffering. It's a vicious circle. You must do more to make things right, but the more time you spend on something, the less time you have to spend on other things which in turn must be perfected.

Overjoyed and underworked

Now doesn't that sound good? Of course, if you are doing work you enjoy it seems a lot less like work anyway.

Is there enough joy, satisfaction or fulfilment in what you are doing? Did you ever feel you are working so hard but seeing little return, accomplishment or fun? Play, fun, failure and fulfilment are curious and important ingredients. Put them all into a pot, heat them up and see what results you get from your experimentation. Let's hope it goes whoosh! In a good way.

Not everybody works this way. Others seem able to deliver on time and have a life. Do they have a super human intellect? Have they a secret group of worker elves hidden in an office somewhere? Probably 'No' to all the above. At least it is unlikely – especially the last one. There are people who have developed a way of working which reduces stress, increases fulfilment and helps them to get more done more easily.

Playtime

Turning what you once thought of as work into more like play gives you a freshness and a passion that others will find hard to match. I understand if this sticks in your throat a bit. That's why you read about comfort zones earlier. If you can't have fun, laugh, compete and invent while doing what you are doing, you might be a square peg in a round hole. But before you make any big decisions, all it really takes is a change of mentality. You could even think to yourself, 'I am going to really enjoy this. I'm going to enjoy the challenge, the struggle and the opportunity to grow – to excel.' When you reframe your outlook it will transform your life.

Having this perspective will mean you are far more comfortable with change than most. It's important that you are because achieving your potential will involve many seasons of change. It never stops for you or the organisations where you work. Change should be seen as possibilities to be realised rather than a disruption to be resisted.

Change or die

Studies in America discovered that people would rather die than change. That is, they'd sooner risk severe medical conditions than exercise and eat more healthily to improve their life expectancy. What's new there, you might ask. But this is not just anyone. The survey was of people who'd suffered seriously because of poor health already. In fact they'd had heart surgery. Heart surgery doesn't mean you won't get another heart attack; it means it will relieve the constant pain, but it's only a lifestyle change that will really protect you.

In some cases their condition was so severe they could hardly walk a few metres, and couldn't even make love because of the pain. Literally 90 percent of patients who'd had heart surgery because of health problems were found to prefer to keep their old lifestyle, vastly increasing their risk of death or repeat surgery and possibly both. The lifestyle changes needed are all the old favourites: smoking, too much drinking and eating, not enough exercise and too much stress. It's not just their health that's at risk. These procedures cost in excess of $100,000 each time.

How can it be the case that people who appear to have such a strong incentive to change still don't change?

Don't stand still

At a corporate level, and depending on which report you believe, somewhere between 60 percent and 80 percent of change initiatives do not achieve the objectives they set out to accomplish. If $100,000 sounds expensive, imagine the cost of failure for these abortive change initiatives.

What does this mean for someone like you? Are you going somewhere? Guess what there will be plenty of along the way? Change. In fact it will be almost constant because settling is no longer an option in a global marketplace that is developing as quickly as it is.

Change is unsettling, worrying and demanding. It's also exhilarating, inspiring and renewing. If you are on a mission to make your contribution, be fulfilled, effective and rewarded for it, then you will need to keep growing, learning and changing. You'll also need to reframe, adjust, reposition and at times revolutionise what you are doing and the way you do it. Change is not the domain of a few specialist change managers or consultants. It's your domain and you need to know how it works and what counts.

Not learning about change will keep you on the launch pad without a clue how to make progress. Change is a skill and an art that can be learned and used to achieve your goals. If you do learn it you'll move much more quickly than those who are behind the curve, and you'll shoot past others who have atrophied in their current state.

Knowing is not enough

I listened to an interview with George Clooney. As well as asking him about his acting career, the interviewer referred to his involvement in international advocacy and humanitarian assistance in Darfur. The interviewer made the assumption that because of Clooney's fame and access to the media it made it easier for him to cause things to change. Clooney replied, 'Knowing something doesn't change anything. If knowledge changed anything doctors wouldn't smoke.'

You may have heard the phrase, 'burning platform' used in the context of change. Literally meaning that if you are on an oil platform and it is on fire you are going to take some radical action. The problem with that example is that few situations in life and work are as drastic or as black and white. What's clear about that example is that both your mind and emotions are highly focused and energised because the situation has changed so drastically.

Choose change

Don't wait for it to be so bad that you absolutely must do something about it. Most people wait for change to be thrust upon them, and then find themselves in the situation of being forced to change by others or by circumstances. That's why people find it easier to make a career-changing decision when they've been made redundant. You'll need to notice what needs to change, initiate movement and create dissatisfaction and hope in others. You need to be sensitive to more subtle clues and indicators.

In *Switch,* Chip and Dan Heath suggest three important aspects of change to be worked on at the same time. The analogy they use is of a Rider on an Elephant following a Path, which they developed from *The Happiness Hypothesis* by Jonathan Haidt. Because we are emotional and rational beings and we get tired we have to work on them all at the same time...

1. Direction for our rational brain
2. Motivation for our emotional brain
3. Shape the situation to make it as easy as possible

Many change writers and practitioners advocate developing the business case, and there's no doubt that it is important for us to be convinced by the rationality of the argument. However, you and others have to be prepared and motivated in other ways. The point is that our rational side is not as powerful as our big ugly emotional side. That's why it's easier to reach for another cigarette, chocolate bar or glass of wine when you are feeling blue or stressed compared to doing some exercise which will get those endorphins flowing and pep you up in a much healthier way.

Spot the difference

But there are times when we embrace change enthusiastically.

Even when it gets hard we persevere. Moving house, changing jobs, getting married and having children are all incredibly disruptive events, but we do them with joy and energy despite the challenges they can represent.

Think about changes that you have voluntarily made. What was it about them and you that made you go ahead? You didn't just do it when you had no other option. You actively planned for it. I know everyone has their impulsive moments, but it was probably a combination of these things that meant the change was successful.

- ✓ You had a strong desire and/or dissatisfaction
- ✓ It made sense to you
- ✓ It felt right
- ✓ You were enthusiastic and/or determined
- ✓ Circumstances favoured it or could be changed to make it possible
- ✓ There was a good level of support from others
- ✓ You worked out how to do it
- ✓ You began to see yourself and your situation differently
- ✓ You persevered when there were setbacks and found another way forward
- ✓ Problems or resistance from others involved were overcome through listening, persuading and negotiation
- ✓ You celebrated the steps along the way

Change challenges

If change isn't happening, something is missing. Look at the list above and ask yourself what's missing.

The *Switch* model explains three reasons for lack of progress:

- What looks like **resistance** is often lack of clarity (Direct the Rider)
- What looks like **laziness** is often exhaustion (Motivate the Elephant)
- What looks like a **people problem** is often a situation problem (Shape the Path)

This means:

1. If it's not really clear where you need and want to go, you'll encounter resistance.
2. If you and others aren't motivated you could just be tired of initiative after initiative.
3. Before you focus on changing people's behaviour try changing the situation to make change easy and straightforward.

Don't bite off more than you can chew

You tend to be really optimistic and overambitious at the beginning of any change projects. When the realities of the difficulty, or complexity of the change becomes more obvious then enthusiasm and performance drop off and lots of change initiatives fail at this point. It's illustrated in what's known as the classic change curve.

It may seem a bit counter-productive, but experience tells us that if you set off with a slightly lower ambition in the first place you are likely to achieve greater improvement in the end. Why? Because you don't get stuck, discouraged or worn out in the middle. Better to set a realistic ambition and achieve more than aim too high and miss altogether. When you are an expert perhaps then you can bend the rules, but in the meantime it is sound advice.

The secret to lasting success is persevering through the ups and downs. Don't try to change everything at once. Choose one chapter or skill from this book and really put it into practice. See what difference it makes. Choose something easy to start with. Pick the low-hanging fruit, not the piece that is hardest to get at. Each little victory, each progress step will give you more energy and excitement to learn and implement even more.

BIG MENTAL NOTE

If you are over concerned with doing it right you'll put the brakes on adventure, creativity and imagination.

| ONE SMALL STEP |

Change your mind. Change is good. Change is essential.

---

19 | THINK

Stretch your mind and make your brain big

Man's mind, once stretched by a new idea, never regains its original dimensions.

OLIVER WENDELL HOLMES

Think in more than one direction

Early in my career I had a boss who always seemed to come up with new ideas. By the time I'd got used to how we were going to do something he'd already come up with a different way of doing it. We'd be travelling together, having the sort of business-oriented discussions you have when you are on the road, and he'd be proposing a new way of doing things whilst I was still implementing the last set of ideas.

It was infuriating and exhausting. My brain would be working overtime trying to work out how we'd incorporate the alterations and changes. What would I say to the staff? What about all the money we'd just spent on the new system? That person has only just taken on that role – we can't move them yet!

Slowly it dawned on me.

What for me sounded like a concrete change that needed to be implemented was for him a way of free-thinking. He'd look ahead, backwards, sideways and every other direction to explore alternative and perhaps better ways. He'd discover things happening in completely unrelated sectors and wonder if it could be applied to ours. He'd think about different parts of the organisation and come up with ideas for how they could be developed.

It took me a little time to catch on, but after a while I realised how he kept coming up with all those ideas. He spent time thinking about them. He'd take time to do it by himself and when he was with me he was often simply thinking aloud.

Don't watch your step, look where you're going

A friend of mine was training for a marathon and did his training early in the morning. One day he arrived at work with a huge lump on his head and a blackening eye. He had run into a lamppost. He had been so fixed on watching his step on the ground immediately in front of him he'd not looked where he was going. Ouch! Your concern to be surefooted could be much more costly in the long run because you simply do not see the opportunities or threats ahead.

If you take an advanced driving course, one of the main things you work on is greater awareness and improved observation. It's all about being aware of what could happen around you and what other road users are doing and might do. That's what makes you an expert. It helps you to respond to the unexpected and make timely decisions. Lampposts are unlikely to leap out into the road, but unpredictable critters like children or cyclists wearing dark clothes and not using lights at night (yes, it is a bugbear of mine) might.

If you want to be one of the best players, you have to learn to read the game. You can't just do your bit; you have to see what is going on around you. You have to see the bigger picture. This is what makes someone stand out as better than the rest. It's almost funny watching a player who is brilliant at weaving around the opposition only to find himself down in the corner without having passed the ball to the strikers who could score. All the skill and dedication suddenly becomes rather pointless.

Plenty of people are good at their bit. You can become so engrossed you become blind to other opportunities and changes. The trouble is, you can be so good at your bit you get defensive about it. You become resistant and inflexible. You keep doing things the way they've always been done, but the competition is moving on. The game has changed. What worked then won't work now. To stay ahead you have to stand out and, if you think like everyone else and go along with the crowd, you don't.

It's better to have some of the questions rather than all of the answers

Every organisation that is competing internationally needs everyone to engage in continual improvement of their processes, products and services. But that's not the whole story. You have to see yourself as a global player in an international marketplace. Just because someone is sitting the other side of the world doesn't mean they are not a threat or an asset. It's not up to your company to engage you, it's up to you to engage yourself. They are only one of the companies you will work for. Your outlook needs to:

1. Be bigger and wider than your own role and department
2. Encompass the trends and developments shaping your industry or sector globally (because it really is a small world)
3. Watch the horizon for the gate crashers who'll spoil the party
4. Habitually disrupt the status quo
5. Look to the fringes of your industry – new rules are written at the edge

There are some mighty tomes about strategic thinking that make it all seem rather intimidating. The problem with strategic thinking is that it can be divorced from strategic action. That's where you come in. Combine this quality with others in the book and you'll have them eating out of your hand. I often hear the plea from senior people that others would see the bigger picture. Seeing the bigger picture is not enough: turn it into meaningful challenge and effective action. If you develop the habit of questioning your assumptions, norms and conventional wisdom, you'll be well on the way.

Mess with your mind

Of course, you could leave all this thinking to someone else. It's not easy blazing the trail. You could hide in your shell, keep your head down and not rock the boat. Hold on, another cliché will come to me in a minute. But that's the problem: we are awash with clichés and business speak, which is why it's so hard to break out of the patterns that control our perspectives.

When a new quartz technology was developed by Swiss Nationals and offered to the industry, Swiss manufacturers refused to embrace the technology resulting in *The Swiss Watchmakers Crisis*. The number of employees fell from some 90,000 in 1970 to 30,000 by 1984, and the number of companies decreased from 1,600 in 1970 to 600. Texas Instruments in the United States and Seiko in Japan developed the quartz watch and demolished the Swiss hold on the market, reducing their share to just 10 percent in three years. Your successful past can block the door to an even more successful future.

My boss (the one with all the ideas) had developed a way of messing with his mind that enabled him to come up with ideas and daydream – all perfectly legal as far as I know. He once told me how he'd lie down and put on some relaxing music and then set his brain a problem as he drifted near to sleep. This is when he found new ideas came to him. This is similar to Thomas Edison's method.

Edison would settle into a comfortable chair and nap. On the table in front of him he would place a pad of paper. In each hand he would grip a steel ball bearing, and on both sides of the chair he would deposit a metal plate. He'd then sit back in his chair, dangle each hand over its respective plate, and doze off to sleep. As he began to drowse, one or both of the bearings would fall out of his hands and hit the tin plates, waking Edison with a start. It was in that period of half-waking, half-sleeping that many new ideas came to him.

Have you ever had that experience of a solution popping into your head when you've almost stopped thinking about the problem or you are doing something completely different? This is why you get good ideas in the shower or when you are dropping off to sleep. Make sure you write them down. The subconscious has a way of rewarding that kind of co-operation.

What is it that is seemingly impossible today, but if you could do it would fundamentally change your business or your life?

Think customer

I was in a leading high street store a few days ago, waiting to pay for a few items, and there was a lengthy but friendly exchange between one of the checkout people and two customers. It became apparent that the checkout woman had made a lot of effort to make the system controlling her checkout machine do things it wasn't really designed to do in order to solve a problem for them. She said, 'The problem is, the people who design these never come to the shop to see how it works for the customers.'

If you become too remote from what is important for your customer, whether they are internal customers or external customers, your success will be threatened. Think about one of the typical experiences you have when you expect great service – going to a hotel for a weekend in the country, for example. When did you last do it?

When did the experience start? Was it when you checked-in or before?

The first factor in your experience could be visiting the website of the hotel. How easy is it to find your way around the site? Have they thought about all the information you, as a customer, could need? Are there photos of the bedrooms? Is there a menu? Have they described places of interest? There's so much that makes a good hotel website. How easy is it to book? Did they send a prompt confirmation?

This is the first part of your customer experience and it will begin to form your impression of the place. What's next?

Imagine you are driving into the grounds of the hotel. Is the sign from the road easy to see? Is it clean and freshly painted? How about the grounds? Are they attractive and well kept? Does it all live up to expectations or do the photographs on the website seem to have come from somewhere else entirely?

Now you are walking up to reception. What are your first thoughts? Is the foyer welcoming? Is the receptionist friendly, helpful and efficient? Does it live up to the promises made by the website? Is it well cared for or is it getting a bit tatty?

Next you'll go in the lift, down a corridor, into your bedroom and check out the bathroom. You might ask for room service or visit the restaurant, and every step along the way you'll be making judgements about whether it lives up to its claims and if it's good value and what you'll tell your friends. Did it make your day or ruin your weekend?

Each little experience along the way contributes to the reputation and success of your chosen hotel.

Spread the love

This all makes sense. You understand this relationship. I am a customer; they provide a service; I pay them. If it's a good service – if it's good value – if it's enjoyable, I will say nice things about them and one day I'll probably go back. It's so easy to write a review, upload a photo and record some video that great feedback can quickly lead to exceptional reputations and success. Of course, it works the other way as well.

Now think about the experience people have when working with you, your team or your company. What are all the different points of contact they have? What will be their experience and how will this affect your reputation, prospects and status? Each time they receive an email, listen to your voicemail message, speak to you on the phone or meet face to face, you are building your reputation.

How do you handle meetings? How reliable are you? What contribution do you make? Are you appreciative? This could be a very long list of questions, so why not think of your own? All you really need to do is think and talk aloud as if you were one of your own customers. What would they say about their experience of you?

Fishy story

At 4.00 a.m. the workers at the world famous *Pike Place Fish Market* in Seattle crawl out of bed and begin another long shift in the open, working with cold, slippery, smelly fish. But when you see these guys at work there's something extraordinary going on. They actually seem to love what they do.

In a memorable little book and video called, you guessed it, *FISH!* film-makers Stephen Lundin and John Christenson together with Harry Paul tell the remarkable story. By watching how they work with each other, how they interact with customers and talking to them about their experiences, the creators signpost four simple principles.

1. **Choose your attitude:** This is what they do every day. As one of them said, 'Will you choose to be impatient and bored or will you choose to be world famous?' If you choose to be *world famous*, excited or positive it will make a huge difference to how you act.
2. **Play**: The fish guys have fun while they work because it is energising and makes work enjoyable. How could you have more fun doing what you do? If it always feels like hard work, the people who are passionate will always be way ahead of you.
3. **Make their day**: This is all about the customer. How does your customer or client feel when they come into contact with you? Do they feel encouraged, helped and energised by something special you do? How can you go the extra mile to make them feel great?
4. **Be present**: Being present means being 100 percent engaged 100 percent of the time. It's especially important for your customers. Have you ever had that experience when you are speaking to someone, but their focus is anywhere except you? This is the complete opposite.

Every relationship counts

It doesn't matter what part of the business you are in or what you are doing; you have customers. Your customers may be your own colleagues. They are called the internal customer. It could be your suppliers. Huh? How does that work? Treat your suppliers as if they are your best customers – see what a response you get. It is a sure fire way of doing a great job and building a first class reputation.

The mistake is when you think you are buried away in the business just doing IT or payroll and you disconnect yourself from the impact of your work on the customers. The customers are the work. It's not the name, it's the mentality. Your customers could be patients or local residents or business partners. Whoever they are, the same mentality has to apply.

I find it strange that people who fall over themselves to help and delight external clients can be difficult and unpleasant with their own team. It makes no sense. You can't deliver a first class service to your external customers if you are acting that way with your own colleagues.

You are used to the concept of providing added value to your clients or customers, but it is so easy to forget that mindset when it comes to colleagues in your own organisation. You wouldn't dream of being late, ignoring or being obstructive to your clients, so why do you do it to your colleagues? You are on the same side. You'd be amazed what an improvement can be achieved in terms of morale, reduced stress and productivity if you start to treat everyone like customers and clients.

BIG MENTAL NOTE

To stay ahead you have to stand out and if you think like everyone else and go along with the crowd, you don't.

| ONE SMALL STEP |

Do a quick audit of all the contact points your customers have with you. What sort of experience do they have? How many stars would you get?

---

20 | SPEAK

Master the power of presenting

Make sure you have finished speaking before your audience has finished listening

DOROTHY SARNOFF

Face your fears

Alison stood up and walked slowly to the front of the group. She looked okay, but it soon became apparent she was literally shaking with fear as she began to give her short presentation. When I say short, I mean six minutes short. Her voice held up for the first 90 seconds, but she was literally overcome with fear by this point and the tears began to flow. Her natural instincts kicked in and she fled the room.

Alison wasn't speaking in front of difficult customers or clients. It wasn't an interview situation. It was a short 'relaxed' wrap up of a development programme she'd attended with colleagues over a 10-week period. There were a few extra invited guests, but no one particularly scary. So what got into Alison? Normally, a level-headed, capable person, but on this particular day she completely fell apart under the pressure of speaking in public.

The session continued as various people spoke about how the programme had helped them in their role. Then the door opened quietly and Alison reappeared. Her makeup was a little smudged and she looked a bit shaky, but tentatively took a seat at the back of the room. I was pleased to see her back because it took some courage to return after leaving the room so ignominiously. Then she really surprised me and everyone else.

As the current speaker finished off and the enthusiastic applause died down, Alison walked to the front of the room before I could announce the next speaker. With me standing by her side she started again. Yes, she was still shaky and no, it wasn't going to win any awards, but she did break through the irrational fear that grips many when it comes to speaking in public. Last time I looked, Alison was alive and well and her career still on track. She survived mostly unscathed, but her mascara had taken a bit of a beating.

You are not alone

Alison is the most outwardly fearful person I have met. Perhaps the others didn't even show up. I know of a professional rugby player who would actually vomit if he was asked to make a presentation. On Saturdays he'd be facing huge 17+ stone, powerful and fast opponents charging at him, putting at risk every bone, muscle and sinew. He knew they'd take every chance to knock seven bells out of him. Put him in front of an audience to speak and he was quaking in his boots.

However you feel about speaking in public, now you are not alone. Wherever you would put yourself on the scale of confidence and effectiveness, this chapter will give you some helpful processes and models to become even better. You need both a measure of confidence and effectiveness. The best speakers have style and substance. I've seen some really enthusiastic presentations that have lacked convincing content. I've also heard plenty of content-heavy talks that leave the audience uninspired and unmoved. This chapter isn't going to analyse all your fears, but it will give you strategies for conquering your fears and honing your skills.

Making your point powerfully and confidently in a way that connects with and moves your audience to action is a key skill for you whatever path you take. Even if you are communicating digitally most of the guidance here is relevant. So let's get to the heart of it.

Greek strategy

As with many of the things you've read in this book, the way you'll really make an impact on others and win them around to your ideas is by having something burning inside you. You will communicate authenticity, excitement and determination through your posture, choice of words, tone of voice, facial expressions and gestures. I'm assuming you're not a great actor – although to present well you will need to come out of your shell and let the best of you come out for others to see.

Remember Aristotle (Chapter 14)? He reckoned that to influence and persuade others you needed to focus on three things Logos (Logic), Pathos (Emotion), Ethos (Credibility). The first two are about the response of the audience and the third is about you. To be effective when you communicate your message and opinions you need all three.

LOGOS

You've got to be able to present your argument logically and with credible evidence to back it up. You may think this is what you are doing when you fill your slides with multiple bullet points, tables and graphs. You are not. Over-complicated slides, no matter how impressive the information, will do little for your message and that is what is important after all. Whatever you are speaking about, it needs a clear, easy to follow structure that enables people to follow the argument.

PATHOS

You need to connect with what is important for your audience. This means you have to think about their drivers, worries, hot buttons and hopes. What will move them? Remember the 'What's in it for them?' factor. Presenting is about putting across your message in a way that takes your audience with you because they feel this is all about them and their desires, not you and yours. Most people like to think they decide with cool logic, but the limbic part of the brain where emotion is centred plays an enormous role. If you stand in front of people like a stuffed dummy and speak like an undertaker you'll struggle to connect.

ETHOS

This is all about you. Your reputation will go before you. What's your track record? Have you built up respect and a reputation for delivering results and great customer service? What is it about you that qualifies you to speak on your subject? Have you earned the right to speak? There are many things that can give you credibility. If you are inexperienced in an area you can't invent it, so you have to make sure you've done your research and learnt about the subject and the experience of others. If you are going to apply this wisdom, you'll need to have the confidence to do so, despite the natural nervousness you'll feel. If nerves threaten to turn into anxiety your performance may be affected badly, so here are some golden rules.

Knock out the nerves

Before you talk to your audience the last thing you want to do is talk yourself out of doing well. Follow these invaluable guidelines for dealing with nerves.

1. **It's not about you:** Make a *Big Mental Note* of this one. If you think about a presentation only in terms of your performance, you will mostly be too focused on whether you fail or succeed. Instead, think about it as an opportunity to help and serve others. You may be helping them understand a problem, make a decision, improve a process and many other challenges.
2. **Visualise:** You can talk yourself out of success simply by over-imagining failure. The truth is what you make it. So see yourself doing well in your mind's eye. See yourself being fluent, calm and engaging. See yourself coping if something goes wrong. See your audience listening intently and enjoying what you have to say.
3. **Practise:** Beginning well is key, because once you get going you'll probably get into your stride. Practise your opening in front of the mirror. Smile.
4. **Get them involved:** A good way to calm the nerves is to get rid of the 'us and them' feeling by involving your audience. Start with a simple 'show of hands' question and raise your own. Then move on to something they can nod or say yes to. Then ask a simple open question to someone who has appeared responsive.

5. **Be yourself:** Regardless of all this advice there is no one, perfect, business-speak way of doing presentations. Relax and aim to enjoy it; presenting can be really enjoyable. What an opportunity to make a mark and build your reputation. Don't rush at it – the floor is yours.

The majority of people who listen to you will want you to do well. They may be listening because they have to, but on many occasions they will have chosen to give up their precious time to come to listen to you. You need to do your best to prepare a talk that adds value to their day, week or year and maybe their lives. Yes, it can be done. Being adequate is not enough. Being an inspiring communicator is one of the best ways to boost your cause or career.

Get ready to be great

Becoming skilled at presenting can add a load of fun into your personal enterprise, whether as an employee or a business owner. Seeing people respond to your ideas and give it the big thumbs up is a great feeling – much better than a little polite applause or, worse still, stony silence. You may still be on the starting blocks when it comes to presenting or, like most people I know, you have your way of doing things, for better or worse. Wherever you feel you are you can get to the next level.

P.R.E.P.A.R.E. embraces all the key elements for success. Use this method so that you can confidently deliver any presentation, whatever the situation.

- ✓ Propose – What is the main purpose of your presentation? What outcome do you want? Make sure you state it early without giving away the whole idea so that people know why they are in the room. Time-starved senior people appreciate knowing early on where you are going. Build up their sense of anticipation.
- ✓ Recognise – Identify the people who will hear your talk. What are their hot buttons? A good way to think this through is to ask yourself, 'What are their…
  - Fears?
  - Interests?

- Frustrations?
- Ambitions?

What is the mix of personality types? What you communicate (Substance) and the way you communicate (Style) should be guided by your answers to this.

- ✓ **Engage** – Create an opening that has *impact*. The first few moments of a presentation will be key in forming impressions and getting the full attention of your audience. How are you going to draw them in? How will you make them take notice of you and what you have to say? Hello my name is… can be dispensed with quickly then give them a great reason to listen to you. This could shock, intrigue, surprise or impress them.
- ✓ **Profit** – What will be the overall profit or advantage of your proposals? How will you quantify it? What's the bottom line? What will the audience and the people they represent gain? What pain will they avoid? This must be pinpoint accurate. It must scratch where they itch. It must give them a sense of relief or anticipation. It must solve a problem or fulfil a desire.
- ✓ **Action** – Develop your Main Points. Three is usually enough and each should have this structure.
  - **Proof**: This is the information that will persuade them of the logic, credibility and reliability of your proposal. You can use a story, conclusions from statistics (what story do they tell?), a demonstration of new equipment or technology, expert opinion or similar.
  - **Action**: What do you want the audience to do? What is your 'Call to Action'? All too often you inform the audience, but you do not say what you want them to do. Be crystal clear about the response you want.
- ✓ **Repeat** – Conclude your presentation by concisely summarising the main Call to Action. Dale Carnegie said 'Tell the audience what you are going to say; say it; then tell them what you've said.'
- ✓ **Ending** – Finish with a memorable punch line. It should be so memorable that if they forget everything else about your presentation they'll remember this.

Different people have different styles. You don't need to become a super extrovert. Whatever your style, you need to develop the skills that will enable you to connect to your audience to persuade, excite, and influence. It's one of the chief ways that you will get support and resources. It's one of the ways that you'll spur people to action whether in team briefings, public arenas or managers meetings. Whether you are presenting to potential investors, prospects or your boss it's essential you learn to make your words count. It's one of the ways that you'll keep yourself moving up in the right direction and doing what you want to do.

BIG MENTAL NOTE

You'll really make an impact on others and win them around to your ideas by having something burning inside you.

| ONE SMALL STEP |

Take the stress out of presenting by using P.R.E.P.A.R.E. Once you have a reliable system then you can be yourself.

---

21 | ZOOM!

Why stay on the launch pad when you could be in orbit?

Always be a first rate version of yourself rather than a second rate version of somebody else

JUDY GARLAND

Accidental accountant

It's a little hard to work out how this happened, but one of my first jobs was with an accountancy practice. Somehow I morphed from art student to accountant. Well, I wasn't actually an accountant; I worked in a department giving financial planning advice for their clients. My level of experience and knowledge was frighteningly low. It's scary to think about it now – especially for the clients!

I'd reached the end of my degree and realised that the life of an artist wasn't for me. I also had this blinding realisation that I was going to have to earn some money if I was going to eat. These two insights led me to what was probably a rather hasty decision – I joined a company to sell insurance.

Selling insurance definitely fits in the 'university of life' bracket. It was gutsy work and I learnt a lot about myself and other people. This is where I picked up a little knowledge about pensions, stocks and shares, and insurance, which helped me get the job with the accountants. Oh yes, I was also pretty good at reading upside down, which is what got me through the interview. The interviewer had the answers to the questions about various financial products written on a page and placed in front of him on the desk between us.

Out of the frying pan

It was definitely a relief to get away from the intense, competitive and then mostly unregulated world of insurance sales. However, it wasn't long before I realised that this new world was almost the exact opposite – in a bad way. Everything had to be done in a certain manner. Rules and regulations were coming out of my ears. It was very hierarchical and certain personalities in the office were always right even when they were wrong.

Providing financial planning advice involves writing long letters that demonstrate understanding of the client's tax situation. My manager had a very idiosyncratic way of writing letters. Unfortunately, he expected me to be able to write in exactly the same way as him. After countless attempts and numerous drafts covered in corrections I finally had to admit that I couldn't write like him however hard I tried. Trying to correct my style to fit his style was a lost cause. It was like trying to walk in the wrong size shoes. At best, my attempts were clumsy. I just couldn't be him when I put pen to paper.

This is when I started thinking more about what I really wanted to do, where I would fit and what would fit me.

Brand You

In earlier chapters of the book I have suggested you ask, 'What do you want?' Here's another big question, 'Who are you?' I was introduced to the phrase 'Brand You' in Tom Peters' little gem of a book by the same name. In his unique style, Peters' sends a wakeup call to knowledge workers. Writing in the 90's, he recognised the growth of the knowledge worker and the loosening of ties between big companies and their employees. Instead of having the luxury of nestling in the security of the name of the big company, more and more executive level people would find themselves moving job much more regularly than before.

Coca-Cola, Nike and BMW are brands. You are used to thinking about them that way. You can probably quote their strap lines and remember a few adverts. If you were asked what they stand for, whom they appeal to and what some of their unique qualities are, your answers will probably be reasonably accurate. That's because these companies work extremely hard on positioning themselves in the marketplace. Everything about their look, product, price and reputation management are crafted to ensure that they appeal to the customer they want to appeal to.

A few years ago, Gap spent considerable sums developing a new logo, only to find their customers didn't like the new look. Brands build up loyalty, trust, emotional attachment and meaning. Customers feel they have a stake in the brand and, in return for their commitment, they expect consistency and reliability.

So what's your brand?

If you were a brand, what would people be buying? Let me change that. You are a brand: what are people buying when they buy you? Professional networks like LinkedIn have made this type of thinking more normal for some – at least for those who have caught on. You now live in a global marketplace. Even if you are not planning to up sticks and work anywhere else in the world, the people who consider hiring you have a global market to choose from. I recently walked into the central London offices of a client specialising in engineering consultancy and was amazed to see so many Asian faces as a proportion of those in the open plan office. This was very different from just 18 months earlier.

What a great opportunity, especially if you know who you are and what you uniquely offer. It's not enough to have letters after your name or even an impressive sounding job title. What you need is the evidence of what you have done. 'You are only as good as your last project,' is one of Peters' mantras. What have you done and how have you done it? But achievements are only part of the story. The way you go about it, your personality, voice and tone – as they call it in brand speak – are also hugely important.

Blow your own trumpet

This could be a new way of thinking for you, but it is vitally important. Recently I was coaching a senior executive who needed to present the purpose of her role to the board during a reorganisation. Scary stuff. They were asking questions such as 'Why does your job exist?' and 'What value does your role add, specifically?' Have you noticed this shift? That you are expected to build, deliver and articulate the value of what you do. You can't just sit in the role and assume that everyone around will automatically consider you indispensible because that role has always existed or even because it seemed like a good idea last year.

Don't panic! A mistake that you can make is taking for granted the things that you are good at. I'm good at speaking, motivating and encouraging. I am good at facilitating groups to solve problems and develop motivational goals and plans. I'm good at quickly explaining problem-solving tools in a way that accelerates idea creation. I am good at applying these things with groups that have apparently conflicting priorities. I do this regularly and I am familiar with it – and that can mean I take my skills for granted. You do many, many things well. Just because it is your day job doesn't mean it's insignificant. Value what you do well, learn to articulate it in dynamic language and others will take notice.

How does who you are fit with who you want to be? Think about the gap and what you need to do to fill it. What market do you want to be in and how close are you to fitting the bill? Closer than you think.

Distinct or extinct

How are you different from all the other people in your sector or industry? What makes you more buyable? What special talents, experiences, knowledge and personality create the wonderful blend that is you? You are unique. No-one else has what you have. Yes, you need to keep learning and growing, but make sure to 'Be yourself'. This phrase has tended to sit on the shelf alongside 'I need to find myself' – and there is really nothing wrong with either. It's not airy-fairy gobbledegook. Can you see now that being yourself is vitally important to your career, your future, and your happiness and fulfilment?

How long do you feel like you've been ducking and diving, bobbing and weaving trying to be someone else's idea of you? You've spent too many years waiting for other people to define you or the job to define you. If you are going to be different from 95 percent of the people around you, selfishness is a necessity. A little bit of narcissism will take you a long way. I hereby give you the freedom to indulge yourself for a change. Take some time out and think about who you really are. This isn't about navel gazing; this is about building your brand.

Admiring and emulating the qualities of others make an important contribution to your development. There's a massive amount to learn from the right people. Copying the successful methods of others is a sensible way to learn quickly. But you cannot be them because you are you and, when you stand in front of the board or present to that client or sit before the interview panel, you need to be confident in who you are, what you stand for and how you add value in your own unique way. You know much more than you realise. The next step is to articulate it and own it. Throw out false humility – believe in yourself and get to work!

BIG MENTAL NOTE

If you were a brand what would people be buying? Let me change that. You are a brand. What are people buying when they buy you?

| ONE BIG STEP |

Begin developing your brand.
Why? – Why do you exist? What's your passion?
What? – What is your special product or service? What are you known for? What do people appreciate about what you do for them and the way you do it?
How? – How do you stand out from everyone else? How do you leave people feeling?
Who? – Who are your customers? What are their needs and wants?

STOP - GROW - FLOW Chart (3)

PART THREE

Chapters 14-21

Review each chapter and make a quick note of a thought or page number under each heading. Don't write too much. The trick is fewer notes but more action.

STOP (What do you need to stop doing?)

1.
2.
3.
4.
5.
6.

GROW (What new ways of doing things do you want to begin and how?)

1.
2.
3.
4.
5.
6.

FLOW (These are your ideas for making good practices a lifelong habit)

1.
2.
3.
4.
5.
6.

THE AUTHOR

Chris Wisdom has had a rich career, during which he has sold insurance, run two small businesses and headed up communications for an international not for profit organisation.

He's been a motivational speaker, project manager, consultant, executive coach and trainer. Throughout this time, and using hundreds of hours of interviews, he has studied, researched and identified the habits, attitudes and skills that make people successful at work, especially in large, complex organisations.

In the last five years Chris has synthesised this experience in the *Boost!* message and at the same time deepened his research with a Masters degree in Managing Change and Innovation.

Find out more about Chris, or contact him via:

www. wizcomm.co.uk

Twitter: @leadingwisdom

LinkedIn: Chris Wisdom